Setting Up A Strategic Change Management Office (CMO)

Isolde Kanikani

ISBN 978-1-78792-089-7

Book design, layout and production management by Into Print
www.intoprint.net
+44 (0)1604 832149

Contents

Prologue

Why This Book is Needed

The modern business environment is characterized by rapid techno-logical advancements, shifting market conditions, as well as evolving customer and employee expectations. Organizations that fail to adapt to risks losing their competitive edge. This constant flux has made change management a vital organizational capability rather than the pre-2020's assumption that managing change is a nice to have. Structured change management practices ensure that transitions—whether in technology, processes, or culture—are smooth, efficient, and sustainable. However, for change initiatives to succeed, they need more than just reactive approaches; they require strategic oversight and alignment with broader business goals.

The emerging methods of change management need to be streamlined into a lean and value focused approach, we no longer have the luxury to spend more time than is needed, because the next change is always imminently around the corner if not already landing. There is also an exponential acceleration in our understanding of Change Management, a profession that is no longer in its baby shoes but fast becoming mature. Concepts such as Value management, People centred design, Data and performance driven approaches as well as ChangeOps are just a few that we will shed light on in this book. While there are many ways to manage change in organisations, a CMO is presented in this book as a solu-tion and strategy for cohesively managing organisational change and the associated capability. Therefore, the CMO can take many different forms depending on the type of changes being managed, but there is management and orchestration needed to truly reach the aspiration of a change capable organisation, reaping all the benefits that this brings.

Despite the importance of change management, many organizations still struggle with the setup of a Change Management office and once setup, there is often a short life span before these organizational units usually die on their feet. These early renditions have focused too much on the wrong thing, building change management maturity. Losing sight of the very reason for their existence which is to realise strategic goals, an ongoing endeavour that is fuelled by agility and resilience realised by growing organisational change capability.

The key difference between Organisational change capability and Change management capability is that the first is an organisational health factor while the second is one of the tools to realise it. Increasing Change management maturity will increase organisations change capability and with this further enable the organisation to agilely pivot with the requirements of an increasingly volatile market. We will deep dive into this topic in the dedicated chapter, where organisational change capability and maturity are fully examined.

Both the change management and CMO body of knowledge are under developed. We are stepping into exciting times where the management of change is gaining increasing traction, but at the same time there is a need to move away from activity heavy method towards those that truly support return on value from change management and the increasing organisational change maturity when successful.

The movement of organisations to understand the need to fund the setup of CMOs has only started within the last 10 or so years and there are a number of years required before quality insights can be gained from the experience. As such, there is currently a limited pool of knowledge and experience to draw from, making it challenging for new CMOs to establish themselves and deliver repeatable value.

This book aims to fill that gap by providing a structured and detailed guide to setting up and running a successful CMO. To support these pioneers who are often coming from different change management related disciplines. Much of this book is based on my years of experience working with customers on multiple successful case studies, while tying in new thought leadership, research and developments that will also lend themselves to establishing a thriving CMO.

Thank You...

Thanking my husband Fred for his patience given for me to write this book. A special thanks also goes out to all those mentioned below who have peer read this book, your feedback and inspiration are highly valued.

Oana Lazar, Laurens Verberg, Douglas Flory, Martijn Macco, Amanda Foster, Gine Maie

Chapter 1

Introduction

Overview of the Book

The capability to management of change is an essential function in today's rapidly evolving business landscape. Organizations are constantly faced with the need to stay at the forefront of new technologies, market conditions, and internal transformations. These challenging and rapidly changing market dynamics call for diligent and constant monitoring alongside building organisational change capability which is precisely the role a Change Management Office facilitates. This book aims to provide a comprehensive guide on establishing a Change Management Office (CMO), a relatively new concept that has gained prominence in the last decade or so and focuses on the need to build change capability in organisations. By outlining best practices, strategies, and real-world examples, this book will serve as a valuable resource for leaders and management of change professionals looking to set up and maintain a strategic CMO.

"Successful Change Management Office's (CMO) become the strategic heartbeat of business transformation, orchestrating the flow of change and value across an organization. It does not simply manage change—it cultivates the capability for change, ensuring that every initiative aligns with business goals, engages people, and delivers measurable value. A well-designed CMO turns disruption into opportunity, resistance into resilience, and vision into reality, embedding adaptability into the organisation's intrinsic I.D. and DNA."

Importance of Management of Change in Modern Organizations

The ability to manage change effectively is crucial for the survival and success of any organization. Change management involves preparing, supporting, and helping individuals, teams, leaders and organizations in making value from organizational change. It ensures that changes are implemented smoothly and successfully to achieve lasting benefits. The reality in most organizations nowadays is that they are not going through one change at a time, but multiple and with various degrees of disruption. This brings a huge risks like loss of productivity, employee turnover and of not achieving strategic outcomes vital for a healthy and successful organisation.

Where a company might already have active change managers supporting project and portfolio change, a CMO is the difference between Ad Hoc and often operational change to one that is strategic and highly scalable. A well-established CMO can help streamline the management of change, aligning streamlined processes with strategic goals, and ensure that change initiatives deliver the expected outcomes. The set up of a CMO can help organizations become more successful in their change efforts by maturing and improving the overall change portfolio, individual key transformation initiatives, as well as developing the overall change leadership and change management capability of the organization.

A well-integrated CMO also drives measurable business outcomes, optimizing ROI by ensuring that change initiatives deliver sustained value. Ultimately, a CMO transforms change from a challenge into a competitive advantage, embedding agility into the organization's culture and operations. In an era where the pace of change is accelerating, mastering organisational change capability fuelled by a strategic change management practice is quickly becoming a key competitive advantage.

Objectives and Structure of the Book

This book is structured to guide you through the process of setting up a strategic CMO, from understanding its historical context to ensuring its long-term success. Each chapter focuses on a specific aspect of the CMO, providing detailed insights and practical advice. The objectives of this book are to:

- Explore the history and evolution of CMOs setting the foundation for further growing potential for success.
- Discuss how to align the CMO with organizational strategic goals so that the CMO further facilitates these, establishing a

long-term justification for the investment a CMO inevitably requires.

- Highlight the importance of executive sponsorship and ideal reporting lines that are essential to feed the leading strategy of a CMO (so it can further facilitate organisational strategy), have clear and present advocacy for change, and ensure up-to-date alignment
- Emphasize the growth of organizational change maturity as north star over change management maturity as the desired outcome, change management is a tool and means to an end.
- Provide a step-by-step pragmatic guide to setting up a CMO
- Outline strategies to ensure the CMO's strategic success and elevating the practice from what has been, to a setup that ensures CMO remains a vital organisational unit for years to come.
- Describe the important strategic collaborations with other organizational functions

Currently Available thought leadership & a challenge for a more profound approach to CMO strategy and execution

When preparing to write this book, I embarked on a thorough search for all the current thought leadership and practical guidance on setting up CMO's that I could find. This includes the growing body of knowledge and methods specific to change management. But when the focus was shifted to CMOs and organisational change capability, like a number of pioneering topics, there are more high-level perspectives developed in the form of short papers or articles, but less of the down to earth and pragmatic type of guidance that will lead to the repeatable setup of strategically successful CMOs.

There are some commonly shared characteristics brought forward by different sources and also some common misleading combinations of tips, rehashed myths and mixed-up terminologies that do little for helping to setup a CMO. One such example is the 70% failure rate, which when researched lead back to an opinion piece quite some years ago.

Commonly shared characteristics coming from multiple sources include:
- A CMO maintains Change management method, tools and assets
- They develop change capability with executive and senior leadership, usually through coaching or training.
- A CMO is a centre of excellence for Change.
- Provide a community of practice for change managers to share and build on each other's knowledge.
- A CMO manages the people side of change, leaving process, technology and data to other departments.
- Provide consultative support to project teams
- Provide Change management resources on projects
- Track change management progress on projects.
- Track and manage the change portfolio.

Please note that these above characteristics are coming from other sources and not what is being advocated for in the book. This list is a collection of commonly shared CMO associations.

Besides these commonly shared characteristics, there are some great sources taking a more specific approach that does deviate from the norm. HUCMI or Human management Institute does a great job of splitting up the tactical and strategic goals in their article CMO - The change management office (Goncalves), while still relying heavily on the context of project management and PMO collaboration which suggests tactical level capability at best. OCM Solution touches on the topic of CMO's providing an internal service to the rest of the organisation much like Finance or HR, a key highlight that will be exploring later in this book (Airiodion).

A search through the first five pages of Google real Prosci's article on CMOs, Melanie Franklins whitepaper together with articles by Wipro, iTalent Digital and Issoria on the same theme to name a few. Highlights from Prosci's article includes direct quote 'data and experience show that a functional group focused on change management provides value on the enterprise journey to build change management maturity', presenting data collected in their bi yearly published research (Prosci). In the whitepaper, Melanie advocates for 'is a need to understand the scale of change across the organisation, ensure only those change initiatives with the greatest potential for benefits are undertaken' (Franklin). Issoria's article provides tips for sizing the CMO based on the role it plays within the organisation, emphasising the importance of change managers work on initiatives as a good reference for CMO size (Newton, Issoria).

Most sources quote that change management maturity will create a host of benefits for an organisation. This is something I would like to challenge in this book and share a deeper approach, one which includes change management maturity building as a means to the realising organisational change maturity. Change management is a capability and means to an end, building organisational change maturity, a far more profound prospect that requires strategic positioning, multiple mature enough capabilities and a pragmatic approach to truly impact organisations on the scale necessary to realise return on investment.

Who Should Read This Book

This book is intended for a diverse audience, including:

- **Senior Executives and Leaders:** Who are considering establishing a CMO within their organization.
- **Transformation and PMO Directors:** who are looking to incorporate a CMO within their domain.
- **Change Management Professionals:** Who are tasked with setting up and leading CMOs.
- **Project and Program Managers:** Who work closely with CMOs and need to understand their role and value.
- **Organizational Development Practitioners:** Who are involved in fostering change readiness and maturity within their organizations.
- **Students and Academics:** Who are studying change management and organizational development.

Regardless of your role, this book provides the insights and tools necessary to navigate the complexities of change management and establish a CMO that delivers measurable value to your organization.

How to Use This Book

To get the most out of this book, readers should approach it as a practical guide and streamlined reference manual. Each chapter builds on the previous ones, providing a logical progression from understanding the concept of a CMO to strategic positioning, implementing and sustaining it. The chapters also come from a particular angle giving specific information on areas that a practitioner might want to explore in their journey of setting up a CMO. The is the goal to cater for all levels of practitioner including those completely new to the management of change and at the same time tasked with the responsibility to setup a CMO. Readers are encouraged to:

- **Read Sequentially:** To gain a comprehensive understanding of the entire process.
- **Go to Specific Chapters of direct use:** When looking for guidance on particular aspects of setting up a CMO or referencing areas that will be valuable for CMOs already out of the initial setup phase.
- **Engage with Case Studies:** To learn from real-world examples and apply lessons learned to their own organizations.

The book is designed to be both informative and actionable, with practical steps, checklists, and examples that can be adapted to suit the unique needs of different organizations.

Key Takeaways

By the end of this book, readers will:

- Understand the historical context and evolution of CMOs.
- Know how to align the CMO with their organization's strategic goals.
- Recognize the importance of executive sponsorship and optimal reporting lines.
- Be equipped with strategies to enhance organizational change maturity.
- Have a step-by-step guide to setting up a CMO.
- Be aware of critical success factors and strategies to avoid common pitfalls.

- Understand the importance of collaboration with other organizational functions.
- Gain insights into the future outlook and ongoing developments in the field of change management.

Insights into Each Chapter

The aim of the book is to be both a reference point for particular development areas, as well as a comprehensive yet elegant guide to getting a CMO setup. With this in mind, there is an invitation to use the below chapter outlines to support finding input on particular topics.

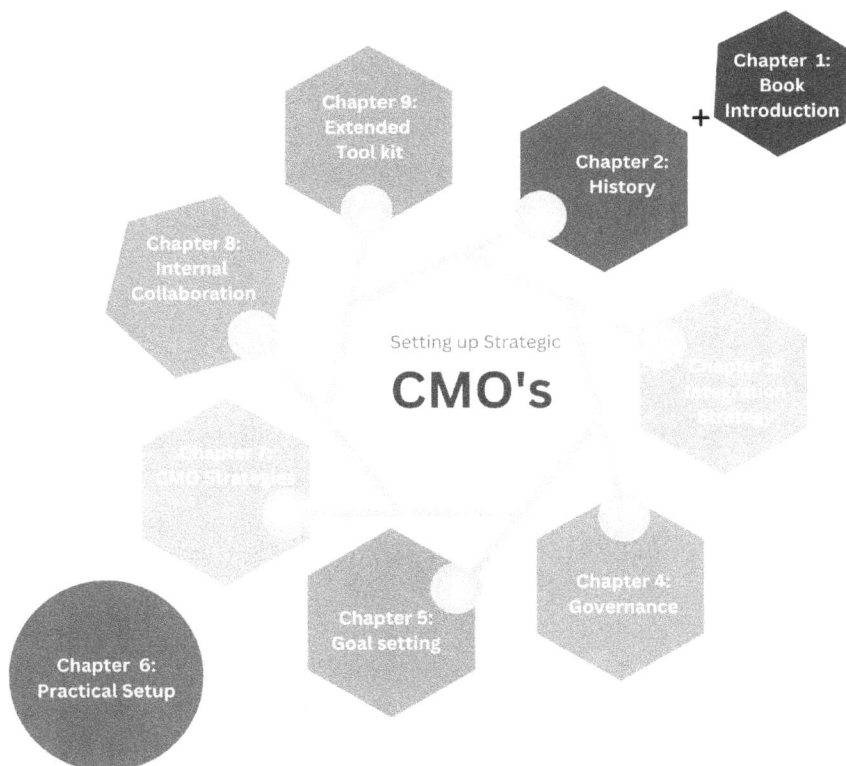

Figure 0: This image shows each of the chapters with chapter 6 highlighted for those who might first appreciate to get a practical basis before deep diving into the more strategic elements of this book. Chapter's 1 and 2 focus on giving a grounding for this book and a 101 guide to topics we will

deep dive into within this book. Ideal for those new to world of managing change, and who would like a basic orientation. Chapter's 3 through to 6 focus on the different aspects of setting up a CMO, with Chapter 6 being the pragmatic quick guide that is augmented by the other three chapters that deep dive into key areas impacting CMO health.

The last chapters extend the tool kit further and target the development of maturity both of the CMO as a new entity and the development of organisational change capability.

- **Chapter 1:** Introducing the what and why of this book
- **Chapter 2:** The History and Evolution of Change Management & the CMO Foundations
    - Provides a historical background and discusses the emergence of CMOs in the last decade.
    - Highlights current trends and challenges, setting the stage for the need for mature change management practices, specifically laying the foundation of what's been done to date in terms of CMO setup and current best practice.
- **Chapter 3**: Aligning the CMO with Organizational design and Strategic Goals
    - Discusses the importance of aligning the CMO with the organization's strategic goals, mission, and vision. It includes case studies of successful alignment and offers practical tips for integration.
    - Practical outcome of this chapter is a strategic business case and plan.
- **Chapter 4**: Governance, Sponsorship and Reporting Lines: Ensuring Effective Leadership and Support
    - Emphasizes the need for executive sponsorship and outlines ideal reporting structures. It details the roles of sponsors and offers advice on building strong relationships with them.
- **Chapter 5**: The goal of building organisational change capability and maturity
    - Differentiates between change management maturity

and organizational change maturity. It provides strategies for assessing and enhancing maturity levels, emphasizing the role of the CMO in this process.

- **Chapter 6**: Setting Up a Change Management Office
  - Provides a step-by-step guide to establishing a CMO, from defining its vision to implementing and monitoring its performance. It includes common pitfalls and how to avoid them.

- **Chapter 7**: Ensuring the Strategic Success of the CMO
  - Outlines critical success factors for CMOs and provides strategies for monitoring performance and sustaining momentum. It includes case studies of long-term successful CMOs.

- **Chapter 8**: **Integration** and Collaboration with Other Organizational Functions
  - Discusses the natural collaborations between the CMO and other functions such as the PMO, Transformation Office, and Value Management Office. It provides frameworks and examples of successful collaboration.

- **Chapter 9**: **The extended** CMO Toolkit
  - Current thought leadership on setting up CMO
  - Exploring various influential methodologies that can be used in CMO setup

- **Chapter 10**: Conclusion
  - Recaps key points, offers a future outlook for CMOs, and provides final thoughts on strategic change management. It encourages continuous learning and improvement.

- **Appendices**:
  - Glossary of Key Terms: Definitions and explanations
  - References listed per Chapter
  - Recommended Readings and Resources: Books, articles, and websites
  - Index: Easy navigation through the book

Encouragement for Continuous Learning and Improvement

Finally, it is important to recognize that change management is an ongoing process. Continuous learning and improvement are key to staying ahead in today's rapidly evolving business landscape. By leveraging the insights and strategies outlined in this book, organizations can build a strong foundation for successful change management and drive sustainable growth. This book aims to be a catalyst for that ongoing journey, providing the knowledge and tools needed to navigate the complexities of change and achieve lasting success.

In conclusion, this book is designed to be a comprehensive resource for anyone involved in or interested in setting up and running a strategic Change Management Office. By following the guidance and best practices outlined in this book, organizations can enhance their ability to manage change effectively and achieve their strategic objectives.

Important terms explained:

There are a number of key terms we have defined below to aid the reader to quickly jump into the contents of this book. A more comprehensive list has been placed at the end of the book, in case you want to reference further terms.

- **Change management office:** This refers to an organised business unit, team or otherwise centrally organised Change capability building focus within a CoE, Transformation office, PMO or HR. In this book, the CMO is used in the broadest and most flexible definition allowing for proper application to any organisation and the specific requirements it might have for change capability building.
- **Change Management:** This refers to both the professional role one can take and the act of managing key changes.
- **Organisational change capability:** This refers to an end of goal of managing change which utilises a CMO, change managers and the building of key organisational capabilities as part of its toolkit.

References:

- Goncalves, Vincente. "CMO – The Change Management Office." HUCMI, HUCMI, 2023, https://change.management.hucmi.com/cmo-the-change-management-office/.

- McKinsey. "The science of organizational transformations." McKinsey, 2015, https://www.mckinsey.com/capabilities/people-and-organizational-performance/our-insights/the-science-of-organizational-transformations.

- Newton, Richard. "How to size your Change Management Office." Issoria, https://www.issoriachange.com/articles/how-to-size-your-change-management-office.

- Franklin, Melanie. "Change Management Office – Benefits and Structure." 2018, https://agilechangemanagement.co.uk/wp-content/uploads/2018/08/CMO-whitepaper-FINAL.pdf.

- Prosci. "The Change Management Office (CMO)." Prosci, 2022, https://www.prosci.com/blog/change-management-office.

- Ottavi, Leslie. "PMO, CMO and TMO: what they are and how they drive change agility." iTalent Digital, 14 July 2023, https://info.italentdigital.com/blog/pmo-cmo-and-tmo-what-they-are-and-how-they-align-to-drive-change-agility.

- Tanweerul Hoda, Mohammad. "How a Change Management office can solve the CIO's ROI Problems." Wipro, March 2021, https://www.wipro.com/consulting/how-a-change-management-office-can-solve-the-cios-roi-problems/.

- Kanikani, Isolde. "CMO: Think big, start small when setting up the Change Management Office!" LinkedIn, 2020, https://www.linkedin.com/pulse/cmo-think-big-start-small-when-setting-up-change-office-kanikani-v1p3e/.

- OCM Solution. "Best 2024 Guide to Establish and Manage a Change Management CoE Read more at OCM Solution: https://www.ocmsolution.com/change-management-coe-guide/." OCM Solution, 2020, https://www.ocmsolution.com/change-management-coe-guide/.

- The Change Compas. "The best organisational structure for enterprise change management." Change Compass, 2023, https://thechangecompass.com/the-best-organisational-structure-for-enterprise-change-management/.
- Kanikani, Isolde. "CMO: What is a Change Management Office?" LinkedIn, 2024, https://www.linkedin.com/pulse/cmo-what-change-management-office-isolde-kanikani-rhfhe/.

Please note that additional references have been added to the above list but not directly used in the text in this chapter. The intention is to share the outcome of research into the topics of CMO setup and Change capability building carried out online.

Chapter 2

The History and Evolution of Change Management Offices (CMOs)

The origins of change management as a formal discipline are often stated to have begun in the late-20th century which also provides the foundation for CMOs. However, some would argue that the roots go even further back, depending on which models have influenced practitioners and how they are recognised. What is important though is to understand the evolution of the management of change and at the same time how unmatured and fragmented the body of knowledge still is. This greatly impacts the setup of CMOs which can still be understood as a pioneer area within change.

Many of the models that we still use today are influencing models from other disciplines, and while very relevant in certain situations they lack some attributes that count them within the change management body of knowledge. Furthermore, they are tailored to fit another time and discipline like sociology, psychiatry and grief cycles. Focusing on individual development which is important but doesn't cater for managing change at scale which our current times ask for.

The development journey of models, approaches and later formed methods is useful to understand so one can make informed choices about which toolkit items are going to bring the value outcomes sought after when setting up a CMO.

The Early Days of Change Management: Influencing models

One of the earliest recognised change influencers is Arnold van Gennep (1909) published a three-step change model, often referenced in discussions of ritual transitions, followed by Lewin, Bridges and Daryl Conner (1970s) that each put their unique spin on the three-step model. These early frameworks highlighted the idea that change involves distinct phases, though it is worth questioning whether these were truly designed as change management tools or if they were solving other problems and later adopted into change practice.

Looking deeper into historical models, Kurt Lewin's three-step model, introduced in 1947, remains foundational to the field. While often referred to as a change management model, it was initially intended to address psychological shifts rather than organizational transformations. Its stages Unfreeze, Change and Refreeze are now applied broadly in managing transitions, though its original purpose was more about unlocking entrenched behaviours to make way for new ones.

There is another family of models that look specifically at the stages of human emotion during transition. Daryl Conners commitment curve (Conner) and the Satir's Change journey based on family therapy, along with others like Elizabeth Kübler-Ross's Grief Curve (1969) later renamed the Change Curve has shaped how practitioners view change as a journey for individuals following tangible stages.

Another significant, though often underutilized, contribution comes from Everett Rogers, whose Diffusion of Innovations theory (1962) introduced a five-step model of change: Knowledge, Persuasion, Decision, Implementation, and Confirmation. This model closely parallels ADKAR and is often seen as a precursor to Prosci's approach. Roger's work, much like Hiatt's, emphasizes the importance of individual adoption in driving organizational success. The methodological depth and close association of Change with innovation management is rarely fully tapped by today's change management community, and could be a vital piece in the benefits story of effectively managing change (Rogers, 1962).

One of the earliest structured change methodologies, La March's Change Model, emerged in the mid-20th century, emphasizing the importance of systematic change interventions. This laid the groundwork for later methodologies, and influenced many a change manager. Don Harrison's Accelerating Implementation Methodology (AIM), which was developed in 1982 as a practical, business-oriented approach to managing change (IMA). AIM focuses on implementation strategies, defining sponsorship roles, and embedding change within business operations.

Beyond traditional models, several innovative frameworks have shaped modern thinking on change. Appreciative Inquiry (AI), developed by

David Cooperrider and Suresh Srivastva in 1987, focuses on leveraging an organization's strengths rather than diagnosing problems, fostering a more positive and constructive change process. Spiral Dynamics, a theory developed by Clare W. Graves in the 1970s, explores how individuals and organizations evolve through stages of consciousness and value systems, impacting how they respond to change (Beck and Cowan). Meanwhile, the Cynefin Framework, created by Dave Snowden in 1999, offers a decision-making model that helps organizations navigate complex and uncertain environments by categorizing challenges into simple, complicated, complex, or chaotic domains ("A Leader's Framework for Decision Making"). These alternative approaches provide a deeper, more holistic view of organizational change, integrating psychological, strategic, and cultural dimensions.

The time when change best practices are established: Birth of Change Management

A more appropriate beginning of modern management of change might be in the 1990s with figures like John Kotter, whose influential article "Leading Change" (1995) and his 8-Step Change Model solidified change management as a strategic business discipline and linear process (Kotter). Kotter emphasized leadership's role in creating urgency, guiding coalitions, and embedding new behaviours into organizational culture. Interestingly, Kotter has since evolved his thinking, moving beyond his 8-Step Model to his "Survive and Thrive" approach, detailed in his book *Accelerate* (2014), which emphasizes agility in a rapidly changing environment (Kotter).

At the same time, Prosci's ADKAR Model, developed by Jeff Hiatt in 2003, emerged as a widely recognized framework, backed by a growing body of research carried out every two years. ADKAR's five stages—Awareness, Desire, Knowledge, Ability, and Reinforcement—focus on individual transitions, underscoring that successful organizational change requires careful attention to how people adapt.

The field has been codified through the ACMP (Association of Change Management Professionals) with the first global Standard for Change Management, published in 2014 and now available in 12 languages.

This global standard has been a key step in formalizing the profession, providing organizations with a comprehensive framework for implementing and managing change across industries. Besides this, the word of the Change Management Institute in driving best practices and certification is also a big contributor to spreading change management best practice globally with the Effective change manager's body of knowledge (The Change Management Institute).

The Six Batteries of Change, introduced by Peter De Prins, Geert Letens, and Kurt Verweire in 2017, presents an integrative framework that balances rational and emotional components of change to ensure sustainable transformation (De Prins et al.).

The following diagram shows the relationship between other organisational disciplines, the previously mentioned influencing models and change management evolution.

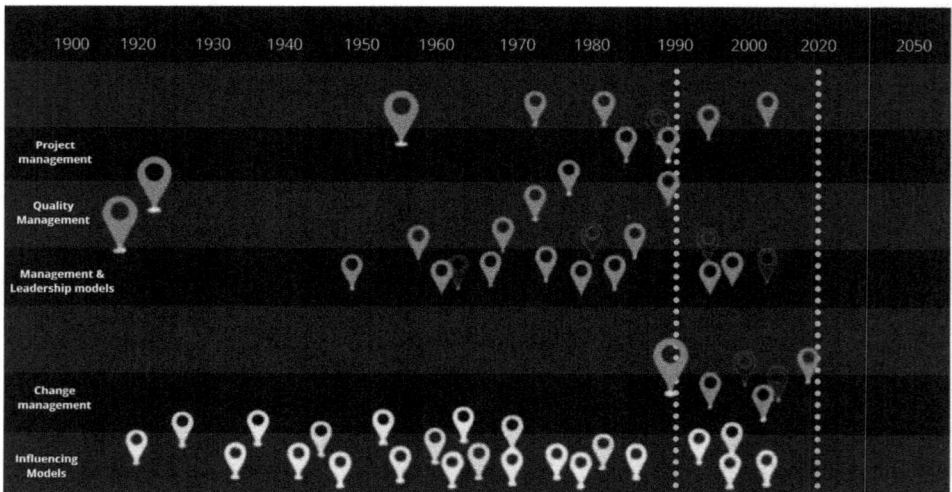

Figure 1: Change Management profession and body of knowledge development Timeline. This figure shows a development time line of different capabilities like project management and leadership put alongside Change management. Besides this the influencing models have their own stream; each yellow marker represents one of 24 well used influencing models that their publish date.

As the field evolves, change management has moved from being a collection of loosely connected activities making use of influencing models to method driven with further work needed to fully fledge in light of the ever increasing a strategic necessity within organisations.

While early models from other disciplines laid the groundwork, the development of dedicated Change Management Offices (CMOs) signals a shift toward a more systematic, scalable approach to managing change in today's complex and fast-paced business environment. There is a growing emphasis on being value and data driven, while managing behaviour change on scale shown by the emergence of new models like the COM-B model (Michie et al.). Where more work needs to be done to develop a value driven and pragmatic way of managing and building change capability in Organisations.

However, as the discipline continues to mature, there remains a gap between the recognition of its importance and the investment required to fully realise the potential of sustainable value from managed change in organizations. Change management is a capability amongst others, that support the develop of organisational change capability. The construct of a CMO is another such tool in the same tool box.

Emergence of CMOs in the Last Decade

The history and maturity of the Change management profession plays a big part in the level of common best practices professionals have to set up a CMO's. While there have been thousands of projects where change management has realised successful results, there aren't so many success stories to date of long standing and thriving CMO's to draw learnings from. Essentially if we are still relatively under developed in our capacity to professionally manage change, we will also struggle to formalise this on the scale needed to set up effective strategic CMO's. Furthermore, the mindset shifts to 'must have 'in terms of change management, puts the profession in a situation that for the first time, it is truly being acknowledged as a key strategic need and player for realising organisational health and market position. But the mindset of investing in this vital area still hasn't caught up with the requirements and the profession actually needs a huge injection of capital to finance real research into best practices development.

The concept of a dedicated Change Management Office (CMO) is relatively new, gaining traction over the past decade. This emergence is driven by the recognition that effective change management requires a centralized, coordinated approach combined with a large increase in the volume of change initiatives. Organizations began to realize that dispersed change efforts often led to inconsistencies, redundancies, and inefficiencies.

In the early 2010s, forward-thinking companies started experimenting with centralized change management functions. These early adopters aimed to create a unified approach to managing change across the organization, ensuring that all initiatives were aligned with strategic goals and executed consistently. As these pioneers demonstrated the value of a CMO, more organizations followed suit, leading to a broader adoption of this model.

The primary drivers for establishing CMOs included:
- **Increased Complexity of Change Initiatives:** Modern change initiatives often span multiple departments and require coordinated efforts.
- **Building Organisational resilience:** A CMO supports employees and customers in changing mindsets and behaviour, important factors in this time of unprecedented number of changes.
- **Need for Consistency:** A centralized approach ensures that change management practices are applied consistently across the organization.
- **Strategic Alignment:** CMOs help align change initiatives with the organization's strategic goals and objectives across siloed departments.
- **Resource Optimization:** Centralized management of change initiatives helps optimize the use of resources and avoid duplication of efforts.

The growing change management need in organizations initiated a new step approximately 10-15 years ago where the first CMO's started to pop up. The average lifecycle of an organisational unit is always extremely reliant on the capability it has to not only help realise strategic goals, but make this tangible. In essence, using data and performance driven decision making aligned to strategic goal realisation is where we need to be.

While some change professionals are extremely capable when it comes to the cutting-edge technology coupled with business case creation that helps create clarity of return on investment from change management. The large majority are lagging behind in the capability to truly make a case for change management using modern tooling available. This is based on the overall figures on data driven and technology driven together with profession specific reports and observations that many in the profession still refer to AI rather or data collection rather than mention specific tools or types of technology in usage (Statista) (Gallop).

Creating a trustworthy data baseline for reporting and a good business case where appropriate does a world of good in terms of helping everyone understand and align around a specified value realisation. That while we make a good amount of impact on one project outcome, there is also a cumulative impact where ROI increases exponentially with subsequent similar projects that can use the same approaches formalised into a Change management best practice or playbook. Making way for a clear place for a CMO to bring value and fund themselves by releasing one-time and cumulative value that would otherwise have been wasted through bad adoption of whatever new behaviours were necessary to make a success.

A nice example is where on one project we speed up adoption releasing one-time value that would have been lost without change management. Put some of the 'won' value back into creating a reusable change play book for further projects creating cumulative return on value. There are also some very tangible ways to map this value in organizations which can be a great addition to the data driven approach and business case creation.

There is also a somewhat unfortunate assumption by many that anyone can do change management. People often get dropped into their first project where they simply have to do the best they can do. Many of the customers I have worked with reached out for advice because of being in such a situation, where upper and C-level management have given them the task of setting up a change management office. In more cases this responsibility is picked up by an experienced change professional, but I have also come across examples where there is no prior change management experience like a hard-core finance consultant or a marketing team lead also taking up the CMO building challenge.

In summary, CMOs have not been high on this list of organisational must haves until recently. Couple this with the low maturity of a collective approach to change management, and the lack of concrete practices that will help drive increased funding, and we have a difficult environment for CMO creation. Once setup, the natural focus toward change management maturity building instead of organisational change maturity means that the lifespan of such an organisational unit is usually pretty short. This is based on the natural reinforcement of a small group of individuals being change capable brought together with the trend of falling into a trap of being too operational and losing sight of driving strategic outcomes.

Current State of CMOs: Statistics and Trends

Despite their relatively recent emergence, Change Management Offices (CMOs) are becoming more prevalent in large organizations. According to a Prosci study, approximately 25% of medium to enterprise organizations have established a CMO or a similar function, with this trend more pronounced in industries experiencing rapid technological change or facing stringent regulatory demands, such as finance, healthcare, and technology (Prosci). In addition to Prosci's data, McKinsey reports that nearly 70% of large-scale transformation efforts fail due to insufficient change management, further emphasizing the necessity for a structured approach like the CMO (McKinsey). Meanwhile, the Change Management Institute found that only 32% of organizations have developed the maturity to manage change effectively, demonstrating the gap that still exists in scaling change capabilities (CMI).

Another key trend involves the new types of change being driven by digital transformation, Environmental, Social, and Governance (ESG) factors, and evolving security requirements. These trends demand more holistic change management approaches, moving away from the traditional project-based, linear methods to more systemic and adaptive models. The emergence of technology adoption roles distinct from organizational change management roles shows a growing differentiation. The former deals with technical implementations, while the latter, which often falls under a CMO's remit, focuses on long-term strategic initiatives like culture change or operational transformations.

Recent developments also indicate a shift toward lean approaches for change management. These lean methodologies focus on value generation and avoid the over-reliance on documentation-heavy methods that were designed for slower, more consultancy-driven environments. The goal is to drive quicker, more effective results with less waste, moving from top-down models to more flexible, distributed ones that empower multiple levels of the organization to initiate and drive change. Agile and hybrid approaches also lend themselves to the same cause, reinforcing iterative change and value creation on the short term rather than putting the riskier waterfall approach into use.

Current trends in CMO development include:

- **Increased Investment:** Organizations are dedicating more resources to CMOs, recognizing the value of structured change management in achieving strategic objectives. However, this investment is still insufficient to develop best practices at the scale needed to deliver organizational-wide change capability.
- **Integration with Other Functions:** CMOs are increasingly aligned with other strategic offices such as Project Management Offices (PMOs), Transformation Offices, and Value Management Offices, creating more cohesion across the enterprise.
- **Focus on Data and Metrics:** There is an increasing emphasis on data-driven decision-making. CMOs are using data and metrics to track the effectiveness of change initiatives and demonstrate their value. These insights not only help guide decision-making but also prove the ROI of change management initiatives.

It is important to note here that there is very little material and data specific to the topic of CMO's, and only a small number of sources exist which is good to take into consideration when taking onboard any facts and figures in this area.

Challenges found in the setup Stage of CMOs

As CMOs are still relatively new, they face numerous challenges in their development and integration into organizations:

- **Lack of Standardized Practices:** With no universally accepted approach, organizations often create their own change management methodologies, which can lead to inconsistencies. A significant issue is the focus on project-based change management instead of strategic, systemic change management. This leads to short-term successes but fails to build long-term, scalable capabilities.
- **Inward-Looking Focus:** Many CMOs fall into the trap of focusing solely on building change management maturity rather than fostering organizational change maturity. This creates a siloed group of change professionals disconnected from the broader business objectives. The key challenge is remembering that change management is a means to an end, not an end in itself.
- **Limited Benchmarks for Success:** With few long-established CMOs in place, there are limited benchmarks or best practices available to measure success and maturity. The profession still struggles to build a clear blueprint for success, especially as the types and complexity of change initiatives increase.
- **Resource Constraints:** CMOs often lack adequate funding and staffing, which limits their ability to operate effectively. This challenge is exacerbated by the growing number of organizational change types being added to the mix—each with its own scale, complexity, and resource requirements.
- **Demonstrating Value:** Proving the ROI of a CMO can be difficult, particularly when the benefits of structured change management are not immediately visible. Securing executive support often requires long-term data and evidence that many CMOs are still in the process of collecting.

These challenges highlight the need for continued development in CMO practices, emphasizing the importance of viewing change management as a critical part of achieving strategic goals rather than an isolated function.

Opportunities for Growth and Development

Despite the challenges, CMOs are poised for growth as the demand for more effective change management increases. The following opportunities can help CMOs drive more impactful change across organizations:

1. **Adopting Advanced Technologies:** Leveraging AI, data analytics, and other technologies can significantly improve how change management initiatives are monitored, tracked, and adjusted in real time. This enables CMOs to predict resistance, measure impact, and optimize strategies based on evidence rather than intuition. New approaches like ChangeOps offer a way to manage different types of change using fit-for-purpose strategies that reduce risk, require fewer resources, and deliver more value. A deep dive into ChangeOps will come in a later section of this book.

2. **Focus on Organizational Change Maturity:** Instead of focusing solely on change management maturity, CMOs should strive to develop organizational change maturity. This means building the capability and capacity for change across all levels of the organization, democratizing the ability to initiate and manage change. This broader focus helps reduce costs across projects, generate a unified approach and generates cumulative ROI capabilities built over time.

3. **Lean Delivery Models:** Moving towards lean change management approaches that minimize waste and maximize value is another significant opportunity. These approaches focus on quicker, more efficient delivery of change, bypassing the bureaucracy that often bogs down traditional methods. The objective is to implement change initiatives that generate real value in the shortest time possible, often using iterative methods that actually drive behavioural change, rather than just administering it.

4. **Enhancing Collaboration:** As CMOs increasingly integrate with other strategic functions like PMOs and Transformation Offices, collaboration becomes more important. Stronger ties across these units can streamline processes, reduce redundancy, and improve the outcomes of change initiatives. CMOs must also collaborate with HR, IT, and other key departments to ensure that change initiatives are seamlessly integrated into daily operations, leadership development, organisation design and culture.

5. **Fostering a Culture of Change:** CMOs can help shape a culture that embraces change by developing leadership capabilities that champion these initiatives. Involving leaders at all levels, rather than relying solely on top-down approaches, fosters a more resilient organization capable of adapting quickly to new challenges. This includes Change Champions and each individual employee that embody change leadership into their everyday way of managing change for themselves and others.

6. **Improve the change management capability:** fostering development a key tool for building organisational change capability. A mature change management capability is one is owned by multiple individuals across the organisation, who understand an optimised approach to realising value through the management of change. The CMI and Prosci Change management maturity models are a good reference point here together with the standard for change management developed by ACMP.

7. **Continuous Learning and Adaptation:** The field of change management is evolving rapidly, and CMOs must keep up with emerging trends, methodologies, and technologies. By continuously learning and adapting, CMOs can ensure they remain relevant and capable of meeting the changing needs of their organizations.

In conclusion, while CMOs face several challenges due to their nascent stage, they also have significant opportunities for growth. By focusing on lean value generation, leveraging new technologies, and fostering collaboration across departments, CMOs can enhance their effectiveness and position themselves as critical drivers of organizational success.

Case Studies: Early Adopters and Lessons Learned

To illustrate the evolution and current state of CMOs, this section presents case studies of organizations that have successfully implemented CMOs. These examples highlight the challenges faced, strategies employed, and outcomes achieved.

Case Study 1: Global Technology Company

A global technology company established a CMO to oversee its digital transformation, specifically focusing on IT transformation efforts. The CMO was tasked with ensuring that all change initiatives aligned with the company's strategic goals, particularly around the implementation of new technologies, such as the ServiceNow platform, which was intended to centralize operations across its IT organization. However, the CMO is still decentralised, with representatives from major regions, including APAC, EMEA, and others. They closely collaborate with the global communications team and the Transformation Office E2E deployment team to implement change initiatives.

Despite being operational for more than two years, the CMO has struggled with a low maturity level. Its primary challenge has been balancing day-to-day operational change management support for ongoing projects, while also trying to maintain and build their own assets and internal practices. Due to the heavy demand for operational-level support, they have not had the opportunity to focus on building out their practice and refining strategic alignment.

Recently, the CMO came under fire when asked by leadership to demonstrate what value they deliver in terms of aligning with strategic organizational goals. While they make a visible impact on managing project-level change, the lack of a clear value framework and the inability to articulate how their work contributes to broader strategic goals made it difficult to justify their existence as a strategic unit. Their challenge lies in balancing operational support with the higher-level mission of aligning change efforts to further facilitate overall business strategy and delivering measurable value. This case highlights the risk of CMOs becoming too operationally focused and not spending enough time on strategic development.

Key Takeaways:
- Regionalized yet decentralized CMO setup that operates in silos, making strategic alignment difficult.
- Struggles with maturity development due to the operational burden.
- High demand for operational change leaves little time to focus on improving CMO practices or creating a strategic impact.
- Difficulty demonstrating clear value to the organization due

to the lack of strategic focus, leading to questions about their contribution to organizational goals.

Case Study 2: Healthcare Organization

A healthcare organization recognized the need for a centralized approach to managing change initiatives, particularly in patient care and regulatory compliance. Initially, the CMO had vague objectives and struggled to create measurable outcomes or justify their contributions. They reached out for advice to establish more strategic goals and align the CMO's vision with core business strategies. Together, we helped them shift from a generic focus to a more targeted approach that clearly supported the organization's primary objectives of enhanced patient care, regulatory compliance, and efficiency in resource use.

This CMO was focused on organizational design, specifically integrating the Rijnlands organisation model and improving the overall operating model. They also implemented continuous improvement initiatives, emphasizing the role-specific training of leadership, nurses, and doctors in change management. A key strategy involved helping medical staff, particularly nurses, not only adapt to but also lead change. For example, nurse circles were created where nurses could propose initiatives for operational improvement. The CMO would then align these suggestions with strategic goals, prioritize them, and feed them back to the nurses for solution development. This approach fostered ownership and engagement among nurses, who are often the hardest group to shift into new behaviours in healthcare settings.

Furthermore, the CMO benefited from CEO-level sponsorship and invested significant time in stakeholder management. By building strong relationships across the organization, they ensured the CMO's initiatives were well-integrated, gaining crucial buy-in at multiple levels. As a result, they developed a robust process for aligning the continuous improvement initiatives of the nurse circles with broader strategic objectives, reinforcing a strong culture of change.

Key Takeaways:
- The initial lack of strategic alignment with the business hampered their early success.
- After realignment, the CMO became instrumental in the proper

integration of a newly established organizational design and driving continuous improvement in line with further realising the organisations goals.

- Nurse-driven initiatives fostered bottom-up ownership of change efforts, increasing engagement and ease of adoption.
- Strong executive sponsorship (CEO-level) and comprehensive stakeholder management were critical to embedding the CMO into the organizational culture.

Case Study 3: Financial Services Firm

Facing significant regulatory changes, a financial services firm set up a CMO to coordinate and manage compliance initiatives. The organization was transitioning from a traditional hierarchical operating model to a service governance and service driven operating model. This shift required a comprehensive approach to managing change, as it affected all aspects of the business, from leadership structures to how teams operated on a day-to-day basis.

The CMO played a crucial role in reducing redundancy by ensuring that all change efforts were well-coordinated. Instead of allowing individual departments to handle compliance in a siloed manner, the CMO introduced a more unified, strategic approach. They aligned all regulatory compliance changes with the firm's new service-oriented governance model, ensuring that the change management processes were consistent, efficient, and in line with the organization's broader transformation efforts.

Through this coordinated effort, the firm successfully minimized operational disruption while transitioning to the new governance model. The CMO's ability to standardize processes and provide a consistent framework for change across the firm ensured compliance with new regulations and smoothed the transition to the new operating structure. Their success was largely due to their ability to navigate large-scale cultural and structural shifts, a task that required both top-down leadership and close coordination with department heads. There was also an important support function where an OCM adviser was made available to support employees receiving new roles and responsibilities. This adviser rand a group campaign to drive role adoption, while also being available for coaching and proactively stepping in where there were clear signs of a role not being properly picked up.

Key Takeaways:
- The CMO effectively managed the transition from a hierarchical model to a service-oriented governance model, ensuring compliance and minimizing disruption.
- Standardized change management processes across the organization helped reduce redundancy and ensured alignment with regulatory requirements.
- The CMO's success was largely due to their ability to coordinate change efforts across multiple departments and ensure that all initiatives supported the firm's broader structural transformation.

These case studies highlight the varied challenges and successes faced by early adopters of the CMO model. From struggling with strategic alignment to balancing operational demand, the organizations learned that CMOs must maintain a clear focus on delivering value to the business by aligning with strategic goals, securing executive sponsorship, and fostering bottom-up ownership of change. For CMOs to thrive, they must not only manage change effectively at an operational level but also demonstrate measurable contributions to the organization's long-term vision and success.

Chapter Conclusion:

In this chapter we looked at the evolution of change management and the influencing thought leadership that has led to the first CMOs being established. The foundations of what a CMO looks like today together with the current challenges many faces have also be laid with some case studies sharing how CMOs in particular industries have been setup together with how differently they can be when managing change.

In the next chapter, the theme will be focused on aligning the CMO to strategic goals and vision of the organisation in order to develop a clear case for initial CMO setup. An aligned business case and strategic plan will often be the very first steps for any CMO getting setup for the first time and important for securing funding.

References:

- Kotter, John P. *Leading Change: An Action Plan from the World's Foremost Expert on Business Leadership*. Harvard Business School Press, 1996.
- Kotter, John P. *Accelerate: Building Strategic Agility for a Faster-moving World*. Harvard Business Review Press, 2014.
- Prosci. "Prosci 12th Edition Best Practices in Change Management." 2022, https://www.proscieurope.co.uk/your-library/prosci-12th-edition-best-practices.
- Rogers, Everett M. *Diffusion of innovations*. Free Press, 1962.
- Satir, Virginia. *The Satir Model: Family Therapy and Beyond*. Science and Behaviour Books, 1991.
- Gennep, Arnold van. *The Rites of Passage, Second Edition*. Translated by Monika B. Vizedom and Gabrielle L. Caffee, University of Chicago Press, 2019.
- The Change Management Institute. *The Effective Change Manager: The Change Management Body of Knowledge*. Vivid Publishing, 2014.
- Michie, Susan, et al. "The behaviour change wheel: a new method for characterising and designing behaviour change interventions." *PubMed*, PubMed, 2011, https://pubmed.ncbi.nlm.nih.gov/21513547/.
- Conner, Daryl. "Building commitment to organizational change." *APA PsycNet*, Training & Development Journal, 1982, https://psycnet.apa.org/record/1982-24560-001.
- Prosci. "5 Levels of Change Management Maturity." *Prosci*, 2025, https://www.prosci.com/blog/change-management-maturity-model.
- Kübler-Ross, Elisabeth. *On Death and Dying: What the Dying Have to Teach Doctors, Nurses, Clergy and Their Own Families*. Routledge, 2009.
- Harrison, Don. *The Change Management Pocket Guide: Accelerating Implementation Methodology (AIM)*. Implementation Management Associates, 1999.

- Cooperrider, David L., and Suresh Srivastva. *Appreciative Management and Leadership: The Power of Positive Thought and Action in Organizations*. Jossey-Bass, 1990.
- De Prins, Peter, Geert Letens, and Kurt Verweire. *Six Batteries of Change: Energizing Change Management*. Lannoo Publishers, 2017.
- Snowden, David J., and Mary E. Boone. "A Leader's Framework for Decision Making." *Harvard Business Review*, Nov. 2007, www.hbr.org.
- Ratanjee, Vibhas, and Ken Royal. "Your AI Strategy Will Fail Without a Culture That Supports It." *Gallup.com*, 1 November 2024, https://www.gallup.com/workplace/652727/strategy-fail-without-culture-supports.aspx. Accessed 2 March 2025.

Chapter 3

Aligning the CMO with Organizational design and Strategic Goals

Organisational design in all its forms lead by the organisations purpose and associated strategic goals are important to work with when setting up a CMO. They provide the guard rails and north star for how our CMO should operate within the organisation. Not taking these into account quickly leads to unmanageable scopes for a CMO and quickly losing sight of the CMO reason for existence, after all a CMO needs to integrate with every part of an organisation to truly realise the bigger goal of growing organisational change capability.

Organisational design differences will impact our rollout strategy and the final shape of our CMO. An example here is that a centralised hierarchical organisation will need a different strategy than a decen-tralised matrix design. Organisational purpose and strategic goals act as another scoping mechanism, and they help a CMO leader to differentiate between work that is waste and work that is relevant. Any form of organisational design is important because if ignored, it will impact your success and can streamline the CMO as a cost centre when aligned. Designs can include goal frameworks, operating models and governance to name a few. These designs or organisa-tional structures offer the stable framework for change, and a place to embed outcomes of changes carried out in the organisation.

We will deep dive into the different scoping mechanisms below in this chapter and the structural implications of above-mentioned structures in chapters eight and nine. The focus of this chapter is looking at how these mechanisms help us scope, align, and setup strategically while having a lean operational approach that doesn't fight current systems.

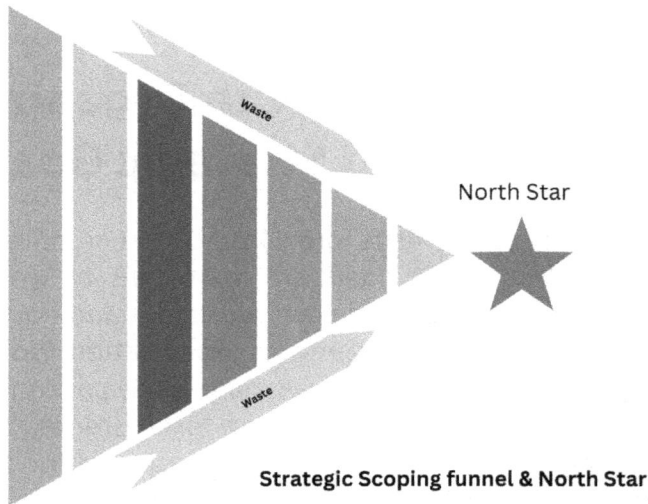

Strategic Scoping funnel & North Star

Figure 2: North start and scoped funnel created limitations of established strategic goals, organisational design and operating model, governance and decision-making structures to name a few. This scoping is incredibly important for the success of a CMO due to there always being limited resources and budget. The more scoped a CMO is and with clear prioritisation system, the more equips it will be to delivery and show value realisation for the organisation.

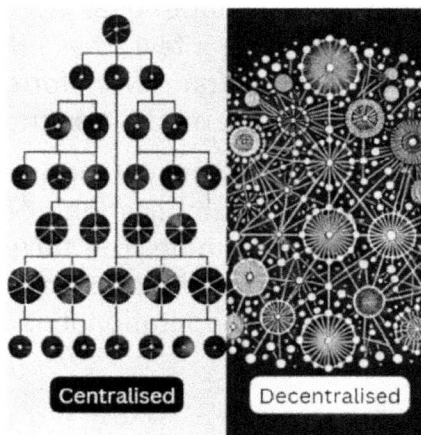

Figure 3: This image shows the difference of centralised or decentralised decision making in organisations which is important to keep into account

when setting up a CMO because there are different strategies that can be good to employ. Centralised organisations tend to opt for one CMO that encapsulates the team, the assets and strategies all in one place. A key C-level sponsor is important and top-down approaches amongst others will need to be used. The risk for a centralised CMO is not getting the right positioning within the often-present hierarchy enough to make strategic impact. Decision making by a small number of key individuals also puts a clear need of leadership and managers management on the table. A decentralised organisation on the other hand, might need a bottom-up approach or one that tailors for different needs. The CMO could be a dispersed team that works together on a remote basis, where a change manager is dedicated to a particular decentralised unit bring best practices. The risk of a decentralised CMO is that scope has a higher risk of becoming an issue together with change management becoming too fractured. Organisational network analysis can be very useful in decentralised organisations to work out a scoped stakeholder management strategy as well as to help

Understanding Organizational Purpose, Mission, and Vision

To effectively align the Change Management Office (CMO) with an organization's strategic goals, it is essential to begin by understanding the core elements that drive the organization: its purpose, mission, and vision. These foundational components shape the organization's identity and provide a roadmap for its activities. The same principles can also be applied to the CMO itself, ensuring that the office is strategically aligned and capable of delivering meaningful change.

Purpose defines why the organization exists, often extending beyond profit to emphasize its core reason for being. For example, a healthcare organization's purpose might be to improve patient health and wellness. Similarly, a well-aligned CMO must understand this purpose and ensure that its own purpose directly contributes to these broader organizational goals. For the CMO, its purpose could be framed as enabling the organization to successfully navigate and implement necessary changes in alignment with the company's long-term vision.

One highly effective method for defining purpose, mission, and vision is Simon Sinek's Golden Circle model, which emphasizes starting with "Why" before moving on to "How" and "What." In this model:

- **Why:** This represents the purpose—the reason the organization or CMO exists. For the CMO, this could mean supporting the organization's ability to adapt to change in order to remain competitive.

- **How:** This explains the process or the strategic approach the CMO will take to achieve its goals, such as using change management frameworks like ADKAR or Kotter's 8-Step model.

- **What:** This outlines the specific actions or initiatives the CMO will implement, such as process redesigns, system upgrades, or cultural shifts.

Applying the Golden Circle to both the organization and the CMO ensures that all change initiatives have a clear purpose and are tied to larger strategic goals. Below is another image showing the cascade of vision that gets translated into mission, values, goals and strategy. Further strategy is then taken into the execution domain where tactics and action plans are created and usually in line with a program or project.

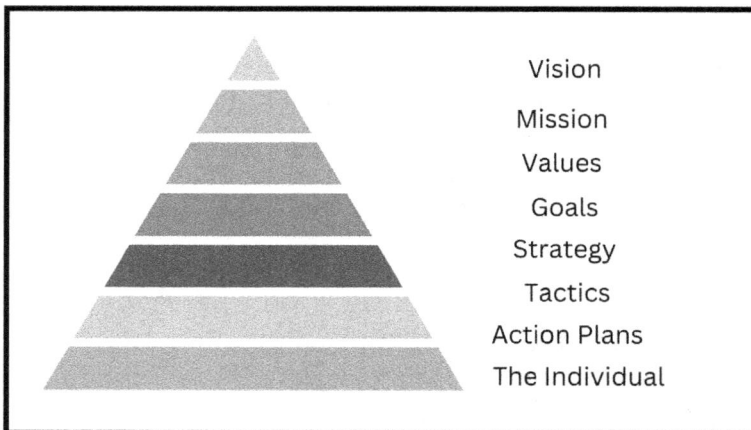

Vision
Mission
Values
Goals
Strategy
Tactics
Action Plans
The Individual

The Strategic Pyramid

Figure 4: This image is showing how there are different levels of focus within an organisation. A CMO needs to be able to align with the Vision, Mission and Values levels. Then facilitate the goals, strategy and tactics levels with change capability building. Last but not least support the practical activities within action plans (project management and change plans amongst others), while driving lasting change at the individual level. The CMO is not simply there to manage the people side of change. It is there to drive change capability for the organisation by supporting properly integrated people and structures that drive organisational value realisation. The CMO needs to operate at every level of the organisation and not get stuck in the tactical and operational (action plans) level where scalability and value realisation will always be minor at best.

Mission defines what the organization aims to accomplish in the short-to-medium term, providing a roadmap for its activities. For instance, a manufacturing company's mission may focus on optimizing production processes to drive efficiency and reduce costs. The CMO must translate this organizational mission into concrete change management actions. This could involve leading change initiatives to automate workflows, reduce waste through Lean practices, or upskill employees to adopt new production technologies.

For a CMO, developing a mission brief or charter can help clearly define its role and scope within the organization. A well-crafted mission brief outlines the CMO's objectives, scope, stakeholders, and expected outcomes, ensuring that everyone involved understands how the CMO contributes to the organization's broader mission. These documents also help a new CMO team to alignment, getting everyone on board with the high-level goals and way the team will be organized.

Vision describes the organization's long-term aspirations, acting as a guiding light for future growth and innovation. A technology company, for instance, might envision becoming a global leader in digital transformation. The CMO must ensure that its change management strategies and initiatives support the realization of this vision. This requires not only aligning individual projects but also continuously reinforcing the overall change journey to keep it consistent with the desired future state.

Similarly, the CMO can establish its own vision to guide its operations. For example, the vision of a CMO could be to become a strategic enabler of transformative change across all departments, fostering an agile and resilient organizational culture. The vision should be ambitious but grounded in the organization's needs and strategic direction.

Tools for Establishing Purpose, Mission, and Vision for the CMO

Several tools can help define and operationalize the CMO's purpose, mission, and vision:

1. Golden Circle Approach: Start by defining the "Why" (purpose), "How" (strategy), and "What" (initiatives) of the CMO.
2. Mission Briefs and Charters: Create clear documents that define the CMO's goals, scope, key deliverables, and success criteria.
3. Strategic Business Plans and Yearly Business Plans: These documents outline how the CMO's activities align with the organization's broader strategy and provide a timeline for key initiatives. The strategic plan focuses on long-term goals, while the yearly plan breaks them down into actionable steps.
4. Business Cases: Develop business cases for specific change initiatives to ensure that each project is justified in terms of cost, resources, and expected value. Business cases also help gain executive buy-in by demonstrating the tangible benefits of change initiatives, including their alignment with organizational goals.

By internalizing these elements and utilizing these tools, CMOs can ensure that every change initiative supports the organization's broader purpose, mission, and vision. This alignment not only facilitates better decision-making but also ensures that change efforts are consistently contributing to the overall strategic direction.

Strategic Goals: Definition and Importance

Strategic goals are measurable, long-term objectives that an organization seeks to achieve to fulfil its mission and vision. These goals shape decision-making and resource allocation, serving as the foundation for the organization's success. Whether the goal is to increase market share, enhance customer experience, or improve operational efficiency, strategic goals provide a clear roadmap for the organization's future.

For a Change Management Office (CMO), aligning its objectives with the organization's strategic goals is essential for several reasons:

- It ensures that change initiatives are directly linked to the organization's strategic direction.
- It helps prioritize efforts and allocate resources effectively, ensuring that key business areas get the attention they need.
- It provides a clear framework for measuring impact, using metrics such as KPIs, OKRs, or other goal-setting frameworks to track progress against business outcomes.

Without a clear connection between the CMO's work and strategic goals, it becomes challenging to justify its contribution to the business. This lack of alignment is a common reason why CMOs struggle to move beyond their initial setup or achieve long-term success.

Integrating CMO Objectives with Strategic Goals

To ensure that the CMO delivers real value, it must integrate its objectives with the organization's goal framework—whether that involves using OKRs (Objectives and Key Results), KPIs (Key Performance Indicators), or another method. These goals must be SMART (Specific, Measurable, Achievable, Relevant, Time-bound) to ensure clarity and trackability across the organization. Here are key steps to align CMO objectives with strategic goals:

1. **Conduct a Thorough Analysis:** Engage with senior leadership to understand the organization's strategic plan. This involves reviewing key documents, such as mission statements, business plans, and existing goals, to ensure that the CMO is focusing on initiatives that truly matter.

2. **Map Change Initiatives to Strategic Objectives:** Once the goals are understood, align key change initiatives with these objectives. For example, if a company's goal is to improve customer experience, the CMO might lead together with PMO the implementation of a CRM system designed to improve service delivery and reduce response times. This direct connection to the organization's strategic goal ensures that the change initiatives are relevant and valuable. High levels of change and project integration are important on the project level and stops CMO input from becoming fluffy and intangible.

3. **Translate Strategic Goals Down the Organization Chart**: It's important to ensure that these objectives cascade throughout the organizational hierarchy. The CMO should work with department heads and teams to translate high-level strategic goals into actionable tasks for lower-level managers and employees, ensuring alignment at all levels. This prevents potential conflicts with other departments or initiatives, such as project management offices (PMOs) or transformation teams, that might otherwise duplicate efforts or work at cross-purposes.

4. **Set Regular Checkpoints for Re-Alignment:** As organizational strategies evolve, regular touchpoints between the CMO and leadership are essential for re-aligning goals. Strategic priorities may shift, and the CMO must remain flexible, adjusting its efforts to ensure continued alignment with the broader business objectives.

5. **Measure Success Using KPIs and OKRs:** Use specific metrics to gauge the success of change initiatives. KPIs might track operational efficiency improvements, while OKRs could be used to set broader strategic targets, such as increasing overall employee engagement in the change process. For example, a KPI might track the reduction in customer complaints after implementing a new CRM system, directly linking the CMO's efforts to the company's goal of improving customer experience.

6. **Avoid Potential Conflicts with Other Departments:** Since CMOs often overlap with roles from departments such as PMOs, Transformation Offices, and Strategy Teams, it's crucial to establish clear boundaries. Developing cross-functional partnerships and conducting regular meetings with these departments will prevent overlapping responsibilities, ensure synergy, and minimize conflicts regarding goal ownership.

By aligning the CMO's activities with these structured goal-setting methods, the office ensures that its contributions are measurable, strategic, and transparent, providing clarity on how each change initiative contributes to the organization's long-term success.

The Impact of Organizational Design, Operating Models and governance

An often-overlooked factor in aligning CMOs with strategic goals is the impact of organizational design and associated operating models. When establishing a new business unit like a Change Management Office (CMO), it is critical to consider how it aligns with the organization's existing structure, governance mechanisms, and operating model. These foundational elements define how work is distributed, decisions are made, and strategic objectives are pursued. Misalignment can lead to inefficiencies, confusion, and ultimately a lack of effectiveness in driving organizational change.

A brief outline of these organisational structures can be understood as follows:

Organizational Design: This refers to the formal framework that dictates the hierarchy, reporting relationships, workflows, and overall structure of a company. Organizational design impacts communication, agility, and the ability to implement change. There are various types of organizational design, such as hierarchical, matrix, flat, or network-based structures, each of which influences how a CMO operates.

Governance: Governance encompasses the policies, frameworks, and decision-making structures that guide an organization's actions. It ensures accountability, strategic alignment, and regulatory compliance. The governance structure affects how change initiatives are approved, monitored, and sustained across the enterprise.

Operating Model: An operating model defines how an organization delivers value by outlining processes, capabilities, and resource allocation. It translates strategic objectives into executable functions, shaping interactions between business units, technology, and processes. A well-defined operating model ensures that the CMO integrates seamlessly into the broader organization rather than functioning as an isolated entity.

Organizational design determines where the CMO should be positioned, how it interacts with other departments, and the degree of autonomy it has in driving change. Whether an organisation is hierarchical or flat, centralised or decentralised will impact the setup of a strategic CMO. For example, a decentralized governance structure may require the CMO to manage changes across multiple divisions, each with its priorities. In contrast, a more centralized organization might enable quicker decision-making but also necessitates a higher level of coordination. Understanding these dynamics is crucial for designing a CMO that can operate effectively across the entire organization. A deeper dive into this topic is done in chapter's seven and eight.

Establishing Important Partnerships

A Change Management Office (CMO) cannot function effectively in isolation. To ensure the successful realization of its goals, the CMO must establish key partnerships with other strategic functions within the organization. These partnerships play a crucial role in creating alignment, fostering collaboration, and enabling the seamless implementation of change initiatives. For a change manager and sponsor, understanding and nurturing these relationships is essential for driving impactful, sustainable change.

These partnerships also play a role in scoping the CMO. There is a big difference between a green field where no transformation office (TO) or PMO exist compared to if these are already established and mature. In the first scenario, the CMO can define itself without having to negotiate with other units and has a lot more autonomy over the strategy for change capability development within the organisation. With a TO or PMO in place, there is both a negotiation and collaboration ended to avoid double work while maintaining clear missions, at the same time there is also an invitation for a much more profound organisational impact if the existing units can work together cohesively.

These key partnerships typically can include:

- **Project Management Office (PMO):** The relationship between the CMO and PMO is vital for ensuring that change initiatives are well-coordinated with project timelines and resource allocations. The PMO manages project delivery, while the CMO focuses on managing the human side of change. By working together, they ensure that change efforts are integrated into project planning, execution, and delivery phases. This partnership helps align project objectives with change management goals, ensuring that changes are adopted effectively by the organization and minimizing the risk of project failure due to unaddressed resistance.

- **Transformation Office (TO):** For large-scale transformations, the CMO must work closely with the TO ensure that change management practices are fully integrated into broader transformation strategies. The TO typically oversees major, enterprise-wide transformations, and the CMO ensures that these initiatives are approached with structured change management methodologies. This collaboration guarantees that transformational efforts are not just operationally successful but are also embraced by employees, thereby maximizing the return on investment of these high-impact projects. Both offices need to align on objectives, resource needs, and timelines to facilitate smooth transitions during periods of significant change.

- **Human Resources (HR):** Since HR plays a central role in talent management, employee engagement, and organizational culture, its partnership with the CMO is essential for preparing the workforce for change. The CMO and HR must collaborate to address potential people-related risks, such as resistance, low morale, or skill gaps that may arise during change initiatives. Together, they can develop training programs, communication strategies, and support mechanisms (such as coaching or mentoring) that help employees adapt to new processes, structures, or technologies. HR's role in managing the employee lifecycle makes it a critical partner for the CMO to ensure that change is accepted and sustained across all levels of the organization. The role of CHRO is an important sponsor supporting the CMO. Couple this with the potential of the CMO to accelerate the implementation of HR Strategic Initiatives, serve as the independent body in assessing the effectiveness of certain people initiatives (non-sensitive initiatives) and constructively challenge the status quo much like an external consultancy but inhouse.

- **Information Technology (IT):** Technological changes are often a significant driver of organizational change. The CMO must work closely with the IT department to ensure that any new systems, tools, or technology platforms being implemented are accompanied by effective change management plans. This partnership ensures that technology rollouts are supported with adequate training, communication, and user adoption strategies. By collaborating, the CMO and IT can mitigate potential disruptions and ensure that employees are equipped to leverage new technologies, driving both efficiency and innovation. There is an important cultural and business mindset shift moving the IT department from the side lines to crucial partner to the business. The CMO can support both the CIO to make this organisational shift through interfacing digital transformation initiatives with the rest of the business.

- **Central Communications:** Clear and consistent communication is a cornerstone of effective change management. A partnership with the internal communications team ensures that all messages related to change are well-crafted, timely, and targeted to the right audience. Whether it's communicating the rationale for change, providing updates on progress, or addressing concerns, the communications team plays a key role in building transparency and trust throughout the change process. By aligning with the CMO, they ensure that messaging supports the overall change strategy, reinforcing key messages that drive awareness and engagement.

- **All function houses and departments**: A CMOs change practitioners can support as internal consultants to the whole organisation. The form this can take is in managing change, positively challenge the way of operating to improve people practices and ensure that organisational debt is eliminated making space for lean operational running and innovation.

Supporting Goal Realization for the CMO

These collaborations are not just about operational alignment, they are about supporting the realization of the CMO's goals. By forming strategic partnerships with key functions across the organization, the CMO can:

1. **Ensure Alignment of Objectives:** Working together with the TO and other departments guarantees that change initiatives are aligned with larger strategic priorities and transformation goals, ensuring a unified approach to organizational change.

2. **Streamline Processes:** Close collaboration with the PMO and other offices ensures that change management efforts are seamlessly integrated into existing workflows, avoiding duplication and inefficiencies.

3. **Reduce Redundancy:** Partnerships with HR, IT, and communications help in reducing redundant or competing efforts, ensuring that all change-related activities are coordinated, complementary, and mutually reinforcing.

4. **Drive Unified, Organization-Wide Change:** By engaging all critical functions, the CMO can ensure that change efforts are not isolated to a single department or initiative but are part of a coherent, organization-wide change management approach. This ensures that changes are adopted by employees at all levels and across all functions, fostering a culture of continuous improvement and adaptation.

Ultimately these partnerships are the driving force for future-proofing the organisational capabilities for the future. for a CMO to achieve its objectives, these strategic partnerships are crucial in building the necessary bridges across the organization. Ignoring above partnership options will likely lead to a struggling CMO and one that can only operationally support change management on projects if it's allowed to remain in existence for any length of time. By collaborating effectively with the PMO, TO, HR, IT, and communications teams, the CMO can create a unified force driving meaningful, lasting change, while ensuring that the organization is fully prepared and aligned to meet its strategic goals.

Understanding Value as an End Goal

One of the key responsibilities of a Change Management Office (CMO) is to deliver value through the management of change. However, defining value is the first and most important step to realizing it effectively. Value can mean different things depending on the stakeholder you're working with, what might be valuable to senior leadership in terms of strategic alignment could differ significantly from what operational teams consider valuable, such as process efficiency or employee engagement. Understanding these nuances allows the CMO to tailor its initiatives and communication to the relevant audience.

Value in the context of change management is not merely about completing projects. Instead, it's about achieving sustainable outcomes that align with organizational strategic goals. This includes measurable improvements in performance, increased efficiency, enhanced customer satisfaction, or the adoption of new processes that deliver ongoing returns. For this reason, value realization must be a data-driven process, where baselines are established that cover goals, success factors, and other supporting data to help the CMO track progress effectively. Setting up these baselines allows for monitoring, reporting, and ongoing adjustments, enabling the CMO to manage change efficiently.

A CMO's success often depends on its ability to scale change management efforts. If the CMO is solely responsible for managing individual projects, it risks becoming overwhelmed by operational tasks, which results in operational-level outcomes rather than strategic impact. To build true organizational change capability, the CMO must find ways to expand its influence across the organization. One method is by implementing a triage model for change initiatives:

- **Simple changes:** Managed by individuals or teams trained in change management, using a self-service toolkit.
- **Moderate changes:** Supported by an Organizational Change Management (OCM) advisor who offers guidance without direct involvement.
- **Complex changes:** Managed directly by a dedicated CMO team member.

This scalable model allows the CMO to focus its resources on high-impact initiatives, while enabling the broader organization to handle simpler changes autonomously. The use of tools such as a change meter or assessment tool can help determine the complexity of each change initiative and allocate the right level of support.

By leveraging such scalable approaches, the CMO moves from being reactive to proactive, helping to build a culture of change throughout the organization while ensuring that its resources are strategically applied. This type of approach to scaling also supports the growth of an internal service structure, where the CMO can gather internal Customer Satisfaction scores and Service level agreements.

Finally, tangible value realization is crucial. This means setting up a baseline that aligns with the organization's goals, outlines key success factors, and provides the data needed to monitor and report on progress. For example, defining a goal to increase customer satisfaction as part of a strategic initiative could include specific KPIs, such as reducing the average response time for customer service. Tracking this data helps demonstrate not only the immediate ROI of a change initiative but also the cumulative impact across the organization as more projects succeed.

By adopting these practices, the CMO ensures that it not only facilitates change but also delivers value that is measurable, scalable, and aligned with the organization's strategic priorities.

Creating the Strategic Business Case and Plan for CMO Setup

Building a strong business case for the establishment of a Change Management Office (CMO) is critical for gaining executive support and ensuring that it receives the necessary resources and time to succeed. The strategic business plan is a great place to practically capture all the different information and outcomes of this chapter. Showing for example how a new CMO will integrate with the business structurally, what value it will bring and how it will bring this value to the organisation.

Strategic Business case components:

- **Purpose**: An internal document that outlines the CMO's long-term direction, growth strategy, and positioning in relation to other internal departments and the way it will input into companywide strategic goal realisation. It is used to align departments, teams, and leadership toward common goals and ensure that business activities support overall corporate objectives.

- **Audience**: Executives, senior management, department heads, and board members.
- **Usage:** Helps leadership teams make informed decisions about resource allocation, market expansion, product development, and competitive strategy over several years.
- **Leads to:** A CMO charter
- **Key Components**:
    - **Strategic Alignment**: Demonstrate how the CMO will support the organization's mission and vision by delivering change initiatives that align with its overarching strategic goals.
    - **Value Proposition:** Outline the tangible and intangible value that the CMO will deliver, such as improving operational efficiency, enabling faster time-to-market, or enhancing employee engagement.
    - **Establish the CMO Identity:** CMO Long-term goals, strategic priorities and value realisation, outline of the CMO integration strategy
    - **Resource Requirements:** Provide a clear breakdown of the resources needed, including team structure, tools, and budget, as well as the expected return on investment.
    - **Risk Mitigation:** Highlight how the CMO will reduce risks associated with poorly managed change initiatives, ensuring smoother transitions and minimizing disruption.
    - **Strategic Roadmap:** Key initiatives and execution roadmap

To fully develop the CMO setup, it is important to establish a comprehensive Business Plan that further develops the above strategic business case. There are two levels of planning involved:

1. **Strategic Plan:** This covers the long-term strategy (3 years as a basic guideline) and growth of the CMO within the organization, further detailing out the strategic business case. It focuses on aligning the CMO with the organization's future direction, identifying key growth areas, and determining how the CMO

will evolve to meet the ongoing change management needs. This plan outlines the broad objectives, projected milestones, and the CMO's role in driving organizational change over multiple years. It ensures that the CMO remains aligned with the company's broader strategic initiatives. A three-step horizon growth strategy can also be helpful for getting key stakeholders onboard with how the CMO will develop the desired business outcomes, showing the natural steps also helps with expectation management.

2. **Annual Business Plan**: While the strategic plan defines the overall direction, goals and growth, the annual business plan is more focused on the short-term execution necessary to achieve the strategic goals. This yearly plan gets into the specific details required to establish budgets, set annual goals, and determine the tactical and operational actions needed. It covers the immediate steps that the CMO will take to realize its objectives for the year, including detailed actions around staffing, budget allocation, project timelines, and operational improvements. This plan is focused on execution of horizon one with elements of horizon two where appropriate.

Business cases augment both the strategic and annual plans by providing further details on particular areas of development and growth that require additional budget and resources. These business cases are essential for justifying investments in specific projects, highlighting opportunities for innovation, and identifying areas that may need targeted interventions to ensure the CMO's success.

A well-crafted strategic business case increases the likelihood of executive backing and continued support. While a dual-level business plan ties the CMO directly to the organization's overall success, while clearly showing how it will achieve this.

Case Studies: Successful Alignment of CMOs

Case Study 1: Financial Services Firm – Strategic Alignment of the CMO

A global financial services firm recognized the increasing complexity of regulatory requirements, digital transformation, and customer experience optimization as key drivers for change. To address these, the firm established a Change Management Office (CMO) that reported directly to the Chief Executive Officer (CEO). This reporting structure ensured that change initiatives were positioned as a core strategic priority rather than an operational afterthought. The CIO was a second major player based on the growth plans for the CMO to become the organisations central transformation office where digital initiatives were high on the priority list.

Aligning the CMO with Organizational Vision, Mission, and Goals: The financial services firm had a corporate vision centred on becoming the most trusted financial institution through innovation, operational excellence, and customer-centric services. The CMO was strategically aligned to these objectives in several ways:

- **Regulatory Compliance Excellence:** The firm faced increasing pressure to adapt to financial regulations such as Basel III, ESG reporting required by new CSDR regulations, GDPR, and anti-money laundering (AML) standards. The CMO ensured that compliance-driven changes were seamlessly integrated into business operations.

- **Digital Transformation and Fintech Integration:** The CMO supported the modernization of digital banking solutions by driving employee readiness for AI-driven automation, real-time payment processing, and blockchain-based transactions. The company also had an inorganic growth strategy where start-up and scale-up fintech companies would be merged giving the organisation vital innovation boosts.

- **Customer-Centric Change Management:** The firm's mission included improving customer experience. The CMO in close collaboration with the marketing team implemented a change playbook focused on digital adoption of new customer service tools, enabling customers to transition smoothly to new banking platforms.

Building a Strategic Business Case for the CMO: To secure executive sponsorship, the CMO leadership developed a strategic business case, demonstrating:

- The cost of unmanaged change, particularly in inorganic growth and compliance-driven changes.
- Projected ROI from structured change management, including reduction in compliance penalties, increased digital service adoption, and enhanced customer retention. Made the additional case for using playbooks that would both standardise change capability, democratise it and build cumulative ROI.
- How change management accelerates technology ROI, ensuring faster adoption of fintech innovations.

Three-Year Strategic Business Plan for the CMO: With approval from the CEO, CIO and Chief Financial Officer (CFO), a three-year strategic business plan was developed to guide the CMO's evolution. The roadmap included:

1. **Year 1: Establishing the Foundation**, defining governance structures, embedding change methodologies into regulatory initiatives, and piloting fintech adoption projects.
2. **Year 2: Scaling the CMO into a full Transformation office**, Expanding the CMO's capabilities to organising the strategic initiatives of the organisation, broader digital transformation initiatives, including AI-driven financial advisory services.
3. **Year 3: Measuring, Optimizing and innovating**, embedding change maturity metrics into enterprise-wide key performance indicators (KPIs) and shifting focus to continuous improvement of the Transformation office embedded within the CMO.

A yearly business plan was also established to ensure that annual budget allocations aligned with organizational change priorities. Regular reporting to the board of directors helped secure continued investment in change management. The years indication used above worked for this particular organisation, and it is good to note that others might need more or less time.

Outcome and Value Realization

- 90% adoption rate of digital banking tools within the first two years.
- Reduction of compliance-related fines by 35%, thanks to improved regulatory adherence.

- Customer satisfaction scores increased by 20%, driven by smoother fintech adoption.
- Foundation for strategic organisational initiative regulation via the setup of a transformation office within the CMO.

Case Study 2: Manufacturing Company – Integrating the CMO with Business Growth Strategy

A global manufacturing company specializing in automation solutions established a Change Management Office (CMO) under the leadership of the Chief Strategy Officer (CSO). Given the industry's increasing focus on supply chain efficiency, digital manufacturing, and sustainability, the CMO was tasked with leading transformational change while ensuring alignment with the company's long-term innovation and growth goals.

Aligning the CMO with Organizational Vision, Mission, and Goals: The company's vision was to become the leading provider of smart automation solutions, delivering efficiency, sustainability, and cost savings for clients. The CMO aligned with this strategic vision by:

- **Optimizing Manufacturing Processes:** The company sought to transition from a make-to-order to a configure-to-order manufacturing model to reduce waste and increase agility. The CMO developed change playbooks for plant operations to help employees adopt this new approach with minimal resistance.
- **Enhancing Supply Chain Resilience:** The firm's strategic mission emphasized supply chain optimization and risk management. The CMO worked closely with procurement and logistics teams to ensure smooth supplier transitions and process automation.
- **Sustainability and Compliance:** With ESG (Environmental, Social, and Governance) compliance becoming a competitive differentiator, the CMO was responsible for embedding sustainability-driven operational changes across production facilities in Europe, Asia, and North America.

Strategic Business Case Development for the CMO: To justify investment in a structured change management function, the CMO leadership prepared a business case focusing on:

- **Reducing operational costs** by minimizing inefficiencies in the existing production model.
- **Accelerating time-to-market** by streamlining process change efforts in manufacturing plants.
- **Managing employee resistance** in transitioning to automated production lines.
- **Ensuring ESG compliance**, particularly in reducing carbon footprint and waste.

The CSO and CFO approved the case, committing a multi-year budget to scale the CMO's impact across all production hubs.

Three-Year Strategic Business Plan for the CMO: Once funded, the CMO developed a three-year strategy to ensure structured and scalable change adoption:

1. **Year 1: Laying the Foundation**: Establishing change frameworks, piloting supply chain transformation, and introducing job-specific change capability training.
2. **Year 2: Expansion & Standardization**: Scaling process standardization and automation across production hubs, aligning change playbooks with Lean and Six Sigma principles.
3. **Year 3: Driving Continuous Improvement**: Embedding change management KPIs into operational excellence metrics, measuring the CMO's contribution to cost savings, efficiency, and ESG goals.

A yearly business plan was also established to ensure that financial planning aligned with change management objectives, ensuring that every change initiative provided tangible business value.

Outcome and Value Realization

- Production lead time reduced by 25%, leading to faster order fulfilment.
- 10% cost savings on raw materials, due to improved procurement change strategies.
- 98% ESG compliance achieved, strengthening the company's reputation with investors and regulators.

Both case studies demonstrate that successful CMOs require more than just operational support, they need a clear strategic purpose. By aligning the CMO with business vision, mission, and strategic goals, organizations can:

- **Secure executive sponsorship** for long-term CMO investment.
- **Develop structured business cases** that justify funding and growth.
- **Implement multi-year strategic plans** to ensure continuous organizational change capability development.

With a well-integrated CMO, businesses can achieve transformational change, improve resilience, and drive sustainable value realization.

Chapter Conclusion:

In this chapter we looked at how organisational structures impact the design and strategy of a CMO when forming. Each type of structure from operating models to vision and mission alignment, offering a way to scope the activities of the CMO. Clear organisational goal alignment, integration with the operating model and organisation design will mean that a CMO can hit the road running rather than fight already established ways of operating.

With strategic alignment, also comes the topic of value. It is vital that a CMO facilitate value realisation and can truly make a case for this for continued sponsorship. There was a method shared for building a strategic business case for initiating conversations on value and funding, taken further into a strategic roadmap and other documents that will help execute.

In the next chapter, the theme will be Governance and how this can be effectively setup to ensure a successful CMO that can navigate between the strategic, tactical and operational work it needs to do to be success. This chapter builds on key themes just covered in chapter three but shares best practices that lead to vital budgeting support, communication flows and clarity of roles and responsibilities to drive forward successfully.

References

- Sinek, Simon. *Start with Why: How Great Leaders Inspire Everyone to Take Action*. Penguin, 2009.

- Hiatt, Jeff. *ADKAR: A Model for Change in Business, Government, and Our Community*. Prosci Learning Center Publications, 2006.

- Kotter, John P. *Leading Change*. Harvard Business Review Press, 1996.

- McKinsey & Company. "The Science of Organizational Change." *McKinsey & Company*, May 2020, www.mckinsey.com/business-functions/organization/our-insights/the-science-of-organizational-change.

- Kaplan, Robert S., and David P. Norton. *The Balanced Scorecard: Translating Strategy into Action*. Harvard Business Review Press, 1996.

- Prosci. *Change Management Methodology Overview*, Prosci, 2021, www.prosci.com.

- Doerr, John. *Measure What Matters: How Google, Bono, and the Gates Foundation Rock the World with OKRs*. Portfolio, 2018.

- Genevieve Kanikani, Isolde. *ChangeOps: Strategically Harnessing All Types of Change to Create Increased Effectiveness and Operational Flow*. 2023, www.irma-international.org/chapter/changeops/332313/

- Bridges, William. *Managing Transitions: Making the Most of Change*. Da Capo Lifelong Books, 2009.

- Collins, Jim. *Good to Great: Why Some Companies Make the Leap... and Others Don't*. HarperBusiness, 2001.

- Drucker, Peter F. *The Effective Executive: The Definitive Guide to Getting the Right Things Done*. HarperBusiness, 2006.

- Hamel, Gary, and C.K. Prahalad. *Competing for the Future*. Harvard Business Review Press, 1994.

- Lafley, A.G., and Roger L. Martin. *Playing to Win: How Strategy Really Works*. Harvard Business Review Press, 2013.

- Rumelt, Richard P. *Good Strategy, Bad Strategy: The Difference and Why It Matters*. Crown Business, 2011.

- Porter, Michael. *Michael Porter's Value Chain: Unlock Your Company's Competitive Advantage*. Bod Third Party Titles, 2015.
- Porter, Michael E. *Competitive Advantage: Creating and Sustaining Superior Performance*. Free Press, 2004.

Chapter 4

Governance, Sponsorship and Reporting Lines: Ensuring Effective Leadership and Support

The establishment of a Change Management Office (CMO) is not merely about creating a new business function—it is about embedding change capability into the DNA of an organization. For a CMO to be truly effective, it must be strategically aligned with the organization's design and governance, furthermore specific leadership alliances will be key to success. Without this alignment, the CMO risks becoming an isolated entity, struggling to demonstrate value, and facing resistance from stakeholders. The long-term success of a CMO depends on three critical factors: integration into an organisation's governance, sponsorship by the right c-level representatives and support for continued driving of value.

Governance ensures that change initiatives are well-structured, compliant, and strategically driven. Sponsorship, particularly at the executive level, provides the authority and visibility necessary for change management to be prioritized across the organization. Leadership alignment ensures that all levels of management understand, support, and actively contribute to embedding change management practices. Something often brought about with the support of a clear sponsor. Without these foundational elements, even the most well-intentioned CMO can fail to drive meaningful and lasting change.

While many governance setups are possible, this chapter will address the most straight forward governance for a CMO with direct C-level reporting and communication lines. Different types of integrations will also be explored later in this book together with key stakeholder groups that need to be engaged if the CMO is to be successful. The below focus on Sponsorship is based on this being a necessary factor in the first step up phase of a CMO, and is in no way implying that a top-down approach to be used as you will read in further chapters.

Importance of Executive Sponsorship

Executive sponsorship is critical for the success of any Change Management Office (CMO). Sponsors provide the authority, resources, and support necessary to drive organizational change. They are essential advocates for change initiatives, securing funding, aligning change efforts with strategic goals, and addressing barriers. A strong executive sponsor can help ensure that change initiatives are seen as organizational priorities, which signals commitment from leadership and encourages employee buy-in.

One popular framework for understanding the sponsor's role is the CLARC model, which emphasizes five key areas of sponsor responsibility: Communicator, Liaison, Advocate, Resistance Manager, and Coach. Effective sponsors communicate the vision and purpose of change initiatives, act as liaisons between various departments, advocate for the initiative at the highest levels, manage resistance, and coach employees through transitions. Another is the SCARF model which is equally good for this purpose but emphasises different pointers. In the end choosing one of the many here that fits with your organisation is the best way to go. Without a sponsor fulfilling these roles, a CMO may lack the organizational clout necessary to enact lasting change.

Ideal Reporting Structures: CEO, CSO, COO or CTO

The reporting line of the CMO significantly impacts its effectiveness. Ideally, the CMO should report to a senior executive like the Chief Executive Officer (CEO), Chief Strategy Officer (CSO), or Chief Operating Officer (COO). The right reporting structure ensures that the CMO has both visibility and influence within the organization, which is crucial for aligning change initiatives with broader business objectives.

There is an often-promoted concept that leaders need to effectively advocate and promote changes for change management to be successful. While this is true for certain types of organisations, having a clear advocate that feeds the capability of the CMO to be and remain strategic is arguably more important because it elevates the whole game of the CMO and not only on a single project. Furthermore, a C-level leader who proactively positions the CMO to fulfil strategic work collaboratively in the organisation means that the CMO is not just informed but mandated to get change done.

- **Reporting to the CEO:** Provides maximum visibility and authority, ensuring that change initiatives are seen as top priorities. This reporting line is best suited for large-scale, transformative changes that require organization-wide alignment.

- **Reporting to the CSO:** Aligns the CMO's activities with long-term strategic planning. The CSO typically oversees strategy development, making this structure ideal for ensuring that the CMO's efforts support future growth and innovation.

- **Reporting to the COO:** Facilitates close collaboration with the operational teams and ensures that change initiatives are embedded in day-to-day processes. This structure is well-suited for operational transformations that impact core business functions.

- **Reporting to the CTO:** CTO in this case refers to the Chief Transformation officer role and would align the CMO with the organisations strategic initiatives, value realisation and directly working on areas that feed organisational strategic goals.

Each of these structures has pros and cons, and the ideal setup depends on the specific needs of the organization and its change initiatives. For example, a technology company undergoing digital transformation might benefit more from reporting to the CEO for broad organizational alignment or a CIO for alignment with IT, while a healthcare organization focused on optimizing day-to-day operations might find reporting to the COO more practical.

A CCO role be the most influential and direct way to connect change to strategy but might take some time before this becomes a common place role. It goes without saying that a Chief Change Officer (CCO) role would also be the simplest way to reflect the importance of change to the health of the organisation by giving Change a seat at the table.

Building a Strong Relationship with Sponsors

Building a strong relationship with sponsors is crucial for a successful CMO. The below notes will be new for some and more of a reminder for others when working with sponsors. To foster this relationship, CMOs should:

- **Communicate the value**: Clearly articulate the benefits of change initiatives and how they contribute to the organization's strategic objectives. Use data-driven insights to demonstrate tangible outcomes, such as increased efficiency or ROI.
- **Regularly update sponsors:** Keep sponsors informed of progress and challenges. Regular check-ins help maintain their engagement and provide opportunities to address issues before they escalate.
- **Seek feedback**: Involve sponsors in key decisions to ensure alignment and demonstrate that their input is valued.
- **Demonstrate quick wins:** Early successes help build momentum and reinforce the value of the CMO's efforts. By achieving and highlighting these wins, the CMO can maintain sponsor support throughout the change journey.

The Change Team and further stakeholders

Besides executive sponsorship, there are many other types of stakeholders to be considered within the organisation. These will depend largely on the scope of the CMO activities and the mandate established together with any other change organising business units like a PMO, HR or a transformation office.

The CMO goals will be tackled in depth in chapter five, and vital collaborations in chapter eight. The composition and importance of the change team that makes up the CMO together with other stakeholders will be further addresses in Chapter six.

Tools and Frameworks for Governance and Stakeholder management

Several tools can support effective clarification of governance at the initial setup stage. These can then be regularly updated based on the speed of organisational development, the amount of strategic level changes and cadence of change capability activities. These include:

- **Stakeholder Mapping:** Helps identify key sponsors and analyse their influence, ensuring that they are engaged at the right level.

- **Organisation Chart (Updated):** An updated organisation chart including the CMO is an important practical outcome for both driving understanding from key stakeholders. This also makes sure this is embedded into the organisations promoted organisation chart driving awareness building and a vital reference point where the CMO is put on the organisational map.

- **Organisational Network analysis:** This might be a bit premature at the early setup stage, but it's a vital tool that can give a lot of information about how the organisation is setup. This can be fed with active data like surveys or passive data the organisation already has. The outcomes inform a tangible data driven approach and is an excellent way to show impact. Mapping relationships or capabilities can be useful, and the suggestion is both with relationships being the most useful in the beginning unless one wants to start immediately working with organisational change maturity.

- **RACI Matrix:** Clarifies roles and responsibilities, ensuring sponsors are accountable and involved in key decisions. This can be used for the CMO in relation to its position in the company, or for more specific areas like change capability building in a program or portfolio that is being worked on. A RACI can also be used to clarify relationships with other business units or departments where there is a high level of cross over in tasks or where there is a grey area which needs to be defined avoiding responsibilities falling through any unseen gaps.

- **Leadership Alignment Tools:** Evaluate whether leadership is aligned with the goals of the change initiative and address any gaps. This can be done with a management analysis where they are assessed on their support for key CMO areas of focus together with the key drivers they have for getting engaged with CMO either as a collaboration or simple support.

Case Study 1: Financial Services Firm – Establishing a CMO in a Complex Banking Environment

A global financial services firm faced mounting regulatory demands, digital transformation pressures, and internal inefficiencies that required a structured approach to change management. To address these challenges, the organization established a Change Management Office (CMO) within its governance and transformation framework.

Governance, Operating Model, and Organizational Structure: The bank operated under a centralized governance model with a matrix operating structure, where business units had regional autonomy but adhered to corporate standards. The organization had a strong risk and compliance culture due to strict financial regulations, meaning any change had to align with governance requirements and risk management frameworks.

Key structural components impacting the CMO setup included:

1. **Governance and Compliance Focus**: Changes had to align with internal risk frameworks, external financial regulations (Basel III, MiFID II), and central bank policies, making structured change management essential.
2. **Matrix Operating Model**: The firm had business units spread across multiple markets with different regulatory landscapes, making change standardization across regions complex.
3. **Existing Transformation Office**: The bank had a well-established Transformation Office (TO) that managed large-scale strategic initiatives, requiring the CMO to closely integrate with it rather than operate independently.

CMO Integration and Alignment with the Transformation Office: Recognizing the interdependencies between transformation programs and organizational change maturity, the CMO was designed as a complementary function to the Transformation Office rather than as a standalone initiative. The two worked closely together in the following ways:

1. **Strategic Alignment with the Transformation Office (TO)**
   - The CMO was positioned as the execution arm for the

people side of change, ensuring that transformation initiatives were not just technical implementations but had structured change adoption strategies.

- The CMO and TO established joint governance, aligning reporting lines and sharing responsibility for transformation success.

2. **Integrated Operating Model**
   - While the TO focused on program execution, IT modernization, and digital transformation, the CMO handled:
     - Change strategy formulation
     - Stakeholder engagement and communication
     - Change impact assessment and adoption tracking
     - Building long-term organizational change capability
   - This structure ensured that every transformation project had embedded change management expertise from the start.

3. **Governance & Reporting Structure**
   - The CMO reported directly to the Chief Transformation Officer (CTO), ensuring strong alignment between transformation goals and change execution.
   - It also had dotted-line reporting to the Risk & Compliance Office to ensure all change efforts complied with governance policies and external regulations.

CMO's Key Areas of Focus: Given the firm's complex regulatory and digital landscape, the CMO focused on three core areas:

1. **Regulatory & Risk Change Management**
   - Ensuring smooth adoption of new regulatory compliance requirements.
   - Supporting teams in navigating cultural and operational shifts caused by increasing regulatory oversight.
   - Establishing a risk-aware change culture within transformation initiatives.

2. **Digital Transformation & Agile Adoption**
   - Driving enterprise-wide digital adoption, particularly AI-driven compliance, digital banking solutions, and IT

modernization efforts.

- Working alongside the Transformation Office to embed agile ways of working across different banking divisions.

3. **Enterprise Change Capability Building**

- Rolling out a structured change management capability-building program, embedding change competencies across the organization.
- Establishing Change Champion Networks in regional offices to decentralize change support while maintaining governance alignment.

Impact & Outcomes of the CMO Implementation

1. **Improved Change Adoption Rates**: By integrating change management directly into the transformation framework, projects achieved an 18% increase in adoption speed, particularly in digital transformation and compliance projects.

2. **Reduced Regulatory Risk**: The CMO's involvement lowered resistance to regulatory changes, ensuring that new compliance policies were implemented on time with minimal operational disruption.

3. **Stronger Organizational Resilience**: The CMO's capability-building efforts improved the bank's ability to manage future transformations, reducing change resistance and increasing leadership engagement.

4. **Scalability of Change Practices**: The CMO's structured approach and close collaboration with the TO created a repeatable framework for managing enterprise-wide change initiatives, making future transformations more efficient and scalable.

Key Takeaways for CMOs in Financial Services

1. **Strategic Sponsorship & Governance Alignment is Critical**: The CMO's reporting line to the Chief Transformation Officer ensured tight integration with transformation efforts while maintaining regulatory oversight.

2. **Embedding Change Management within the Transformation Office Yields Better Results**: Rather than operating in silos,

having the CMO embedded within strategic transformation efforts ensured greater adoption of change initiatives.

3. **A Risk-Aware Change Strategy Helps Drive Compliance:** In heavily regulated industries like financial services, CMOs must align with risk & compliance functions to reduce regulatory friction and increase adherence to change mandates.

By structuring the CMO as an enabler of transformation rather than a separate initiative, the bank successfully built a scalable, governance-compliant, and transformation-ready change function that significantly increased the success rate of enterprise change initiatives.

Case Study 2: Manufacturing Company – Aligning the CMO with Strategic Business Growth

A large global manufacturing company with a complex supply chain and high product customization requirements faced challenges in scaling operations, increasing automation, and improving customer responsiveness. The company was expanding into new markets while modernizing its manufacturing and logistics operations. To ensure these large-scale changes were aligned with business growth objectives, the organization established a Change Management Office (CMO) under the Chief Strategy Officer (CSO) rather than embedding it within HR or Operations.

Strategic CMO Positioning for Business Growth: This strategic placement of the CMO within the corporate strategy function provided several key advantages:

1. **Direct Link to Business Growth Strategy**
   - By reporting to the CSO, the CMO ensured that change initiatives were business-driven, focusing on enhancing operational efficiency, integrating digital technologies, and optimizing the supply chain.
   - The CMO aligned its projects with enterprise-level growth strategies, ensuring all change efforts contributed to long-term business sustainability.

2. **Sponsorship at a Strategic Level**
   - Unlike CMOs placed in operational silos, this setup en-

sured executive sponsorship at the highest level, making it easier to secure funding, stakeholder buy-in, and rapid decision-making.

- The CSO championed transformation efforts across all business units, helping drive top-down alignment for change adoption.

3. **Cross-Functional Coordination**
    - The CSO's oversight helped break down silos between R&D, production, logistics, and customer service, ensuring that change initiatives were fully integrated rather than operating in isolation.
    - Change strategies focused on delivering customer value faster and with higher quality, rather than simply improving internal processes.

Leveraging Organizational Network Analysis (ONA) and Stakeholder Mapping: To accelerate change adoption and maximize impact, the CMO employed Organizational Network Analysis (ONA) and Stakeholder Mapping as key tools.

1. **ONA for Change Leadership & Influence Mapping**
    - ONA helped identify key informal leaders and influencers across different departments.
    - These individuals were engaged as change champions, helping to cascade change messages efficiently and ensuring peer-to-peer adoption of new processes.
    - The insights allowed the CMO to design a change engagement plan targeting the right employees at the right moments to drive momentum.

2. **Stakeholder Mapping to Align Change with Business Needs**
    - The CMO conducted an extensive stakeholder mapping exercise, identifying:
        - Decision-makers and influencers who could support change initiatives.
        - Resistance points where proactive engagement was needed.
        - Customer-facing roles that had direct impact on

- service delivery and satisfaction.
- This approach ensured tailored engagement strategies for different groups, minimizing resistance and maximizing alignment with business goals.

Customer Journey Mapping – Enhancing the Customer Experience through Change: Recognizing that internal process improvements must translate to customer benefits, the CMO integrated Customer Journey Mapping into its approach.

1. **Identifying Key Customer Touchpoints**
   - The CMO worked with sales, operations, and customer service teams to map out key customer interactions along the supply chain.
   - Focus areas included:
     - Ordering process simplifications for better response times.
     - Supply chain visibility enhancements for improved delivery predictability.
     - Automating after-sales support to enhance customer satisfaction.

2. **Designing Process Improvements for Customer Impact**
   - The CMO ensured that process changes directly translated to better customer experiences rather than just improving internal efficiencies.
   - Key initiatives included:
     - Digitizing order tracking, reducing customer support requests by 35%.
     - Automating inventory management, improving on-time deliveries by 28%.
     - Standardizing production workflows, ensuring consistent product quality and 18% cost savings.

3. **Continuous Feedback Loops**
   - The CMO monitored real-time customer feedback on process changes, ensuring that improvements were iteratively refined based on actual market needs.
   - The customer journey maps were updated regularly, en-

suring ongoing alignment between internal operations and external customer expectations.

Key Change Initiatives Led by the CMO: With a data-driven approach and executive sponsorship, the CMO spearheaded several high-impact transformation initiatives:

1. **Automation & Supply Chain Optimization**
   - Implemented ERP upgrades to improve data centralization and supply chain coordination.
   - Automated inventory forecasting, reducing excess stock and improving production efficiency.
2. **Process Standardization Across Global Sites**
   - Developed a standardized production model, allowing faster deployment of new manufacturing plants in emerging markets.
   - Implemented lean manufacturing techniques to improve throughput and reduce waste.
3. **Technology Integration & Digital Transformation**
   - Replaced legacy IT systems with AI-driven analytics for demand forecasting.
   - Integrated IoT-enabled sensors to monitor production equipment and prevent downtime.

Impact & Measurable Outcomes

1. **Increased Operational Efficiency**
   - Supply chain agility improved by 25%, reducing production lead times and ensuring quicker response to customer demands.
   - Standardized workflows resulted in 18% cost savings across production sites.
2. **Improved Customer Satisfaction & Value Delivery**
   - Customer complaints related to delivery timelines dropped by 40%, thanks to improved tracking and automation.
   - Product defect rates reduced by 22%, increasing brand

reputation and reliability.

3. **Enhanced Change Adoption & Resilience**
   - Organizational Network Analysis (ONA) and change champions increased employee adoption rates by 30%, ensuring long-term success.
   - Stakeholder engagement reduced resistance and increased sponsorship participation, accelerating transformation timelines.

Key Takeaways for CMOs in Manufacturing

1. **Sponsorship at the Strategic Level Drives Impact**
   - The CSO's sponsorship ensured that the CMO remained strategically relevant, influencing decision-making at the highest level.
   - This alignment secured necessary funding and resources, ensuring that change initiatives were prioritized.

2. **Customer Journey Mapping Enhances ROI of Change**
   - By aligning internal process improvements with customer value, the CMO ensured that every transformation initiative contributed to real business impact.
   - Customer-centric change led to faster service delivery, improved product quality, and reduced operational bottlenecks.

3. **Using Data-Driven Change Strategies Accelerates Adoption**
   - ONA and Stakeholder Mapping ensured that change efforts were targeted and effective, leading to higher engagement rates.
   - Integrating real-time feedback from customer journey insights ensured that process improvements remained aligned with market demands.

By embedding change management within the core strategic function, leveraging data-driven approaches, and ensuring a direct link between transformation and customer value, the CMO played a pivotal role in future-proofing the company's operations and enhancing business resilience.

Chapter Conclusion:

In this chapter we looked at getting effective sponsorship in place, further securing budget and strategic input on a regular basis needed for the healthy setup functioning of a CMO. Clear reporting structures are crucial for the success of the CMO. By ensuring that sponsors are engaged, aligned, and actively supporting change initiatives, CMOs can drive successful transformations. It's important to highlight that this chapter was establishing the basis of what's needed for setup, and other key stakeholders will be addressed in further chapters but are no less important.

In the next chapter, the theme will be focusing on the goals of a CMO within the bigger organisational vision and mission. Establishing key differences between change management maturity and organisational change maturity. There will also be a deep dive into maturity assessments and one of the key drivers of a CMO which is to build change maturity.

References:

- Beer, Michael, and Nitin Nohria. *Breaking the Code of Change.* Harvard Business School Press, 2000.

- Birkinshaw, Julian, and Jonas Ridderstråle. *Fast/Forward: Make Your Company Fit for the Future.* Stanford University Press, 2017.

- Brown, Reuben. *The Modern Operating Model: How to Align Strategy, Structure, and Execution for Business Success.* Kogan Page, 2022.

- Burton, Richard M., et al. *Organizational Design: A Step-by-Step Approach.* Cambridge University Press, 2020.

- Child, John. *Organization: Contemporary Principles and Practices.* Wiley-Blackwell, 2015.

- Christensen, Clayton M. *The Innovator's Dilemma: When New Technologies Cause Great Firms to Fail.* Harvard Business Review Press, 2016.

- Dulewicz, Victor, and Malcolm Higgs. *Designing the 21st Century Governance Model: Essential Competencies for Boards and Directors*. Palgrave Macmillan, 2021.
- Galbraith, Jay R. *Designing Organizations: An Executive Guide to Strategy, Structure, and Process*. Jossey-Bass, 2014.
- Kaplan, Robert S., and David P. Norton. *The Execution Premium: Linking Strategy to Operations for Competitive Advantage*. Harvard Business Review Press, 2008.
- Mintzberg, Henry. *Structure in Fives: Designing Effective Organizations*. Pearson, 1993.
- Bass, Bernard M., and Ronald E. Riggio. *Transformational Leadership*. Lawrence Erlbaum Associates, 2006.
- Greenleaf, Robert K. *Servant Leadership: A Journey into the Nature of Legitimate Power and Greatness*. Paulist Press, 1977.
- Hersey, Paul, and Ken Blanchard. *Leadership and the One Minute Manager: Increasing Effectiveness Through Situational Leadership*. William Morrow, 1985.
- Heifetz, Ronald, and Marty Linsky. *Leadership on the Line: Staying Alive Through the Dangers of Leading*. Harvard Business Review Press, 2002.

Chapter 5

The Goal of building Organizational Change Capability and Maturity

Building organisational change capability is both the proposed strategic goal of a CMO and a guiding strategy for staying relevant. The building of organisational change capability is the first step for a CMO, with a further vision of building maturity once a basic capability is put in place. This proposed goal is very different to the one more frequently put forward which is to grow change management capability and maturity.

There is a vital difference between organisational change capability and change management capability to be understood here. While the wording difference is subtle, the outcomes are profoundly different. Change management maturity building often ends up with an inward focused CMO that loses sight of value realisation for the organisation, supporting the growth of change capability in a select few that neither speaks to scalability or renewed investment when goals aren't met. Organisational change capability on the other hand creates an outward facing CMO by default, one that is focused on partnership and democratising change capability development. Always keeping its fingers on the pulse of an integrated change capability strategy and roadmap for maturity development.

Furthermore, the development of change maturity as one of the leading CMO goal enables us to measure progress and drive tangible outcomes. With the help of a change maturity framework and model, we can monitor progress of change capability building.

Differentiating Change Management Maturity from Organizational Change Maturity

Change management maturity and organizational change maturity are two distinct but interconnected concepts. Understanding the difference between the two is essential for any Change Management Office (CMO) that aims to move beyond operational project support into a strategic role, where it drives overall organizational transformation.

- Change Management Maturity refers to the maturity of the CMO's practices. It focuses on how well the CMO manages change initiatives, using established processes, methodologies, and tools to implement change effectively. This often involves a core group of change professionals who are responsible for overseeing change on projects. While this type of maturity is critical for executing change initiatives, it can lead to a bottleneck where the CMO becomes overly focused on its internal operations—spending more time maintaining its own practice rather than focusing on the organization's strategic goals.

- Organizational Change Maturity, by contrast, focuses on the broader organization's ability to adapt to and embrace change. This involves embedding change capabilities across all levels of the organization so that change becomes a natural and seamless part of business-as-usual activities. It requires engaging every employee and creating a culture that is open to change, agile, and continuously improving. It also requires building the organizational structures, leadership, and governance frameworks that enable change to happen efficiently and effectively.

The key takeaway is that organizational change maturity is a must-have for any organization that wants to thrive in an ever-evolving business environment. Focusing solely on change management maturity can limit the CMO's potential by confining it to operational-level work.

Organisational purpose
realisation & Effective
governance

Strategic
Purpose & goal
realisation

Value flow
Customers

Innovation &
Organisational
resilience

Operational
Excellence

Transformation
& project
change

Continuous
improvement &
incremental
innovation

Organisational
Change Maturity:
Building organisational capability to
change & realise intrinsic business value!

Driving Change &
Discipline Maturity

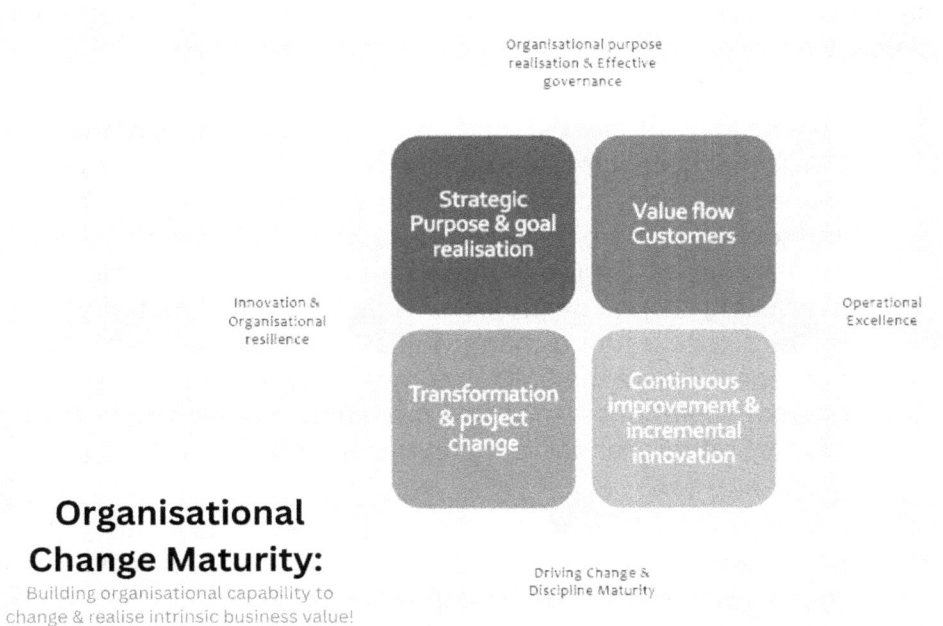

Figure 6: Building Organisational Change maturity model, Isolde Kanikani 2018. This image shows the four focus areas and types of change setting (boxes), with four key change drivers on the outside set as directions. When an organisation seeks to increase value flow to customers, the driving elements of realising organisational purpose and effective governance alongside operational excellence come into to play. Each of the four boxes will be systematically driven by all four drivers, but the related two will often be stronger. A CMO can focus on one box or all four as goal areas.

The Role of the CMO in Maturity Growth

The CMO is responsible for building organizational change maturity. This involves several key actions:

1. Coordinating with Other Departments: The CMO must work alongside other departments, such as the Transformation Office (TO), Strategic Management Office (SMO), and Project Management Office (PMO), to ensure that change is embedded across all areas of the organization.

2. Fostering a Dual Operating System: The CMO should ensure that

change is managed across both the formal and informal networks within the organization. This ensures that both structured and unstructured areas of the organization are aligned and capable of driving change.

3. Creating a Culture of Continuous Learning: Building maturity requires a learning culture, where employees are encouraged to experiment with new ideas and improve their change management skills. This can be achieved through leadership coaching, workshops, and ongoing training to ensure that practices are embedded throughout the employee lifecycle.

Tools and Frameworks for Measuring and Enhancing Maturity

Several types of tools can help organizations measure and enhance their change maturity:

- **Change Capability Maturity Index's and associated assessments:** Provides a comprehensive method for evaluating change maturity across levels, from ad hoc practices to full organizational competency. Aspects of change can be currently measured in assessments like Cultural mapping (Meyer), Forrester's Organisational change management assessment (Barnett), McKinsey 7S and Boston Consulting groups Change Delta model with associated assessment (BCG) to name a few. There is index's available for change management, human resources and other capabilities, and could be dedicated indexes for organisational change capability but these are hard to find.

- **Change capability frameworks:** Universal frameworks give an elegant way to approach the understanding of change capability and through this an associated assessment can be formed. This could be in the form of a decision-making framework like Cynefin, the C+MMF change capability framework, or go in the direction of a change ontology and taxonomy.

- **Change models:** Specific change models can be applied as in assessment form to gage a particular level of capability or simply map change aspects that can be then compared or benchmarked. This could include the older models mentioned in chapter two or new specific models created for the management of change.

- **Change Playbooks:** Custom-designed guides for specific types of change initiatives, like M&A or digital transformation. These playbooks can help the CMO establish best practices, document lessons learned, and scale change efforts effectively. They would also augment any ontology or framework where particular types of change need to be managed to realise optimal value output.

- **Scenario-Based Planning:** Creating scenarios for high-stakes changes can help the organization plan for various contingencies and understand the potential outcomes of different change strategies.

- **Value mapping:** While this seems to go away from the change theme, the ability to map value in organisations means we can further define our strategic usage of limited resources and make a case for continued investment in change capability development.

- **Continuous Improvement and feedback Cycles:** Embedding continuous improvement processes into day-to-day operations helps organizations build long-term change maturity by creating a culture that is always looking for ways to get better. Much of maturity can come down to a data driven approach to monitoring and improving processes, method and approaches. Lean, agile and Six Sigma all offer interesting and well-established approaches to managing change.

This gives a broad over view of the types of tools available for building organisational change capability. We will deep dive into specific tools below and in the Extended tool kit chapter.

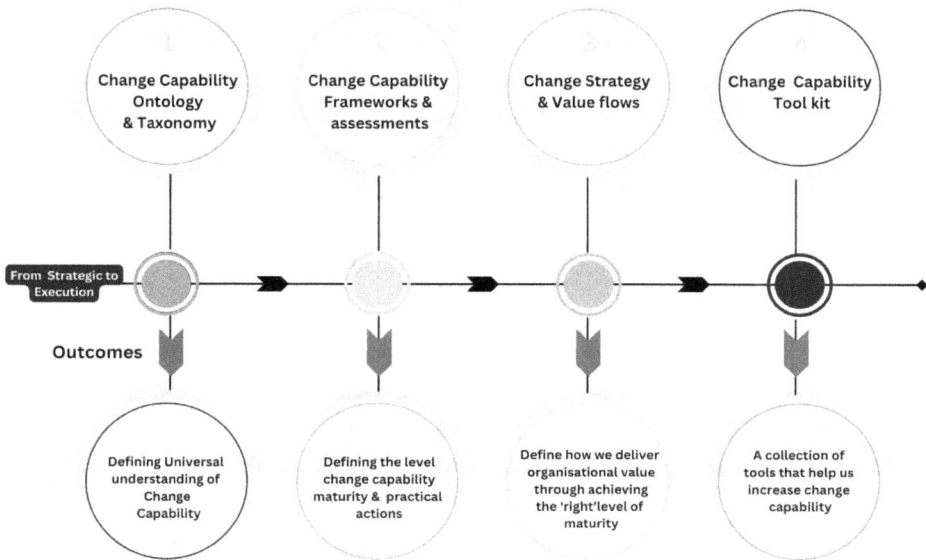

Figure 7: There is a natural cascade of how the above tools and frameworks relate both to each other and the various levels shown in the strategic pyramid. Logically when building change capability, we should start at number 1 in the image above, defining a universal understanding of change capability that elegantly encompasses all other tool kit items will help to create a standard for change capability and through this organisational change maturity development. The green arrows show how tools lead to outcomes, and blue arrows show the direction of building e.g. first we build an ontology with associated taxonomy, then the assessments for capability. Further in the cascade we then assessment the strategic level of maturity we want to reach in order to create value and healthy ROI. Last but not least, building the change capability maturity with new and existing frameworks, methods, approaches, models and others.

Assessing Current Maturity Levels

In the context of organizational change, maturity indexes, models, frameworks, and assessments serve different but complementary roles in evaluating and guiding growth. There is to date, no known change capability ontology or taxonomy that we universally recognise as being the one. There are a number of frameworks, indexes and associated assessments that can be used to gage maturity levels. In order to build organisational change maturity, we need to Keep in mind that building both the key organisational capability maturities as well as the overall change capability is important. Regarding key organisational capabilities like strategy execution, leadership and project management, there are multiple tried and tested assessments that can already be used. Below we will focus on building change capability.

A maturity index provides a quantitative measure, often through scoring, to evaluate where an organization stands on a defined maturity scale. This index shows the level of progress toward specific goals. On the other hand, a maturity model represents a structured path for growth, outlining the stages an organization progresses through as it develops its change capabilities. A framework serves as a broader, overarching structure that provides the guiding principles, methodologies, and practices required to foster growth in maturity. It typically integrates multiple dimensions—like leadership, processes, and culture—into a comprehensive approach. Finally, an assessment is a tool or process used to evaluate the current state of maturity, often using interviews, surveys, or data analysis, providing insights into strengths, weaknesses, and areas of improvement. Together, these tools enable organizations to both understand their current position and chart a strategic course toward greater maturity.

To effectively build organizational change maturity, organizations must first assess their current maturity levels. This baseline will allow for a targeted and pragmatic strategy for growth. There are several well-established tools and frameworks to assess an organization's change maturity:

- **Change Capability Assessment Model (CCAM):** This model takes a holistic approach to assess maturity across dimensions such as strategy, leadership, processes, and culture. CCAM helps organizations evaluate how well they are equipped to handle change across these dimensions.
- **Custom Maturity Assessments:** Some organizations may benefit from customized maturity assessments, tailored to

their specific industry or context. This approach often involves surveys, interviews, or workshops to gather a comprehensive view of the organization's readiness and ability to handle change.

- **Prosci's Change Management Maturity Model (CMMM):** This widely-used model categorizes an organization's change maturity into five levels, ranging from Level 1 (Ad hoc or Absent) to Level 5 (Organizational Competency). It evaluates aspects such as leadership engagement, change management processes, and the degree to which change practices are integrated into the organization's operations and culture. This tool is popular for its structured, step-by-step approach to guiding organizations toward full change competency Management Institute's

- **Change Management Maturity Model:** The Change Management Institute (CMI) offers a global Change Management Maturity Model that assesses key areas like governance, culture, leadership involvement, and skills development. It helps organizations pinpoint specific gaps and opportunities, facilitating targeted growth strategies.

- **C+MMF Maturity Index, Model, and Framework:** The C+MMF (Change Maturity Management Framework) is a flexible and integrative model that accommodates various best-practice models and indexes. It combines organizational ability to change with the structures needed to manage change as part of a holistic strategy to increase change agility. This framework allows organizations to customize their maturity assessment by incorporating other well-known models, thus providing a combined and tailored maturity evaluation. It also emphasizes updating internal processes as maturity increases, supporting the development of higher-level maturity structures. This model is particularly relevant in dynamic or rapidly changing environments, such as those experienced during unprecedented times.

By starting small with these assessments, organizations can identify specific areas for improvement, allowing them to take incremental steps toward building organizational change maturity.

Change Maturity Capability Model (C+MMF)

Factors/ Change maturity levels	L0 Absent or Debt	L1 Ad Hoc	L2 Isolated Change	L3 Interconnected	L4 Org. Standard	L5 Org. Capability	L6 Change mature
Governance & Processes							
Goals, reporting & monitoring							
Roles, responsibilities, compensation							
Systems							
Technology: Tools							
Mindset, attitude, Culture & Beliefs							

Figure 8: Building Organisational Change Maturity C+MMF model & Framework, Isolde Kanikani 2018. This model is a deeply researched change capability and maturity assessment tool. With seven levels designed to flexibly compare all other types of capability maturity in the associated C+MMF framework. Level 0 represents the organisational debt that acts more as a minus to any maturity due to the investment required without value outcomes and a good amount of impact on organisational agility and resilience. Level 7 represents the perfect state of maturity, which is a moving goalpost and focus for innovation as capabilities inevitably development. The majority of established maturity indexes use five levels which directly correlate to levels one to five. There is already a larger body of practice associated with the C+MMF and well worth diving into when seeking to assess organisational change capability.

Practical Steps for Assessing Organizational Change Maturity

Assessing organizational change maturity involves a structured approach to evaluate how well the organization can adapt to change, integrate new processes, and align these with strategic goals. By following a systematic process, you can determine the current state of maturity, highlight areas for growth, and create a roadmap for improvement. Below are the practical steps to assess organizational change maturity:

1. Conduct an Organizational Scan

The first step is to conduct an organizational scan to define the critical areas and capabilities that influence organizational change maturity. This scan should include identifying key processes, competencies, governance models, and strategic priorities that align with the overall health and growth of the organization. Capabilities such as leadership, culture, innovation, and process management are particularly important, as they often indicate how well-equipped the organization is to manage and sustain change.

2. Set Up the C+MMF Framework

Next, set up the C+MMF (Change Maturity Management Framework). This framework acts as a universal connector for various capability assessments that influence the organization's maturity. For instance, alongside assessing change capability, you can also access capabilities like CMMI (Capability Maturity Model Integration), COBIT (Governance and IT Management), ITSM (IT Service Management), and people maturity indexes like those from HRCI or SHRM. By integrating these into the C+MMF, you can create a comprehensive picture of how well each area contributes to the overall organizational maturity.

3. Carry Out Capability Assessments

Using the C+MMF framework, conduct assessments across various capabilities. Each area should be evaluated using its specific maturity model, and then mapped into the C+MMF 7-level framework. This might require adjustments, particularly if some models (like CMMI's 6 levels) or other assessments use different maturity scales. It's good to keep in mind that the C+MMF level 0 is complete absence of capability while level 6 is complete maturity which almost never exists, most 5 step maturity assessments will map to Level 1 to 5 on the C+MMF framework. The C+MMF framework's universal nature helps align these varying assessments into one integrated system.

For instance:

- Project and program management could map at level 4, Corporate governance and goal frameworks at level 3, Knowledge management level 2, Change management at Level 2.
- If a lot of organisational or technical debt exist, then it can be represented by the level 0 in the C+MMF. Level 0 maturity is important to capture as this can have major impacts on all other maturities mapped and definitely impacts the organisations agility and resilience scores.
- Map each assessment to the C+MMF 7-level structure to harmonize the results and compare them effectively against each other. Why do this exercise? We often work with maturity in isolation, neglecting that building in one place often has impact on other capabilities within an organisation and uses up limited resources. The framework allows us to map all key capability maturities alongside each other so we can ascertain where we should invest for maximum effect.

4. Assess the Organization's Strategic Sweet Spot

With the assessment results in hand, the next step is to determine the strategic sweet spot for change maturity growth. This involves analysing the balance between the cost of increasing maturity and the potential ROI. Typically, organizations see significant ROI in progressing from Levels 1 to 3 on maturity indexes, but additional investments for moving to Levels 4 and 5 may offer diminishing returns. By identifying this sweet spot, you can decide where best to focus resources for maximum value realization.

Change Maturity Strategic Sweet Spots & Buffer Zone

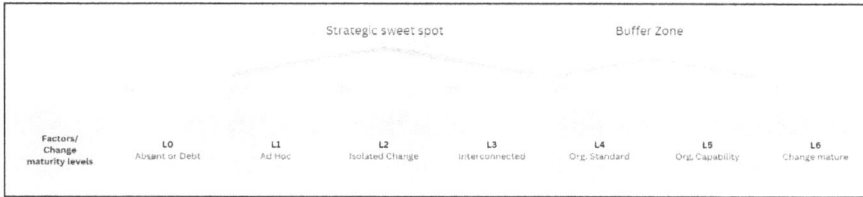

Factors/ Change maturity levels	Strategic sweet spot				Buffer Zone		
	L0 Absent or Debt	L1 Ad Hoc	L2 Isolated Change	L3 Interconnected	L4 Org. Standard	L5 Org. Capability	L6 Change mature

Correlation to Key capability maturity models

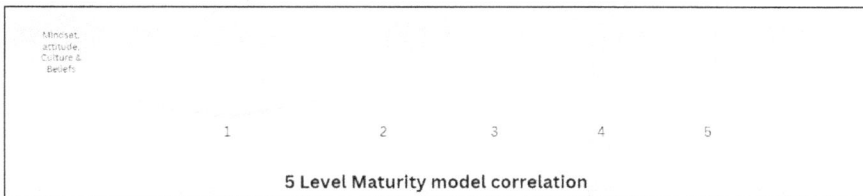

Mindset, attitude, Culture & Beliefs					
	1	2	3	4	5

5 Level Maturity model correlation

Figure 9: This figure shows the strategic sweet spot which refers to the zone that brings the most ROI. Only a few industries and types of organisations will benefit from investing in a level 5, so it's good to clarify the maturity goal the organisation seeks to develop for any capabilities being mapped. The buffer zone represents the area which has questionable value from investment. C+MMF is both a change capability model as well as a framework for working with and assessing the maturity of multiple capabilities alongside each other. This allows for strategic oversight, as well as strategy creation and execution based on assessing vital areas for investment while working with limited budgets. The C+MMF framework allows for already tried and tested maturity models to be directly applied, no matter if they are a 4, 5 or 6 level approach. We can put IT maturity alongside process, project and change maturity as well as any other vital competencies an organisation might want to monitor.

5. Plot the Strategic Sweet Spot on the Framework

Using the data from previous steps, plot the organization's strategic sweet spot on the C+MMF framework. This visual representation will help in understanding where the organization currently stands, where it needs to grow, and which areas of capability should be prioritized for investment and development.

6. Formulate a Strategic Approach to Organizational Change Maturity

Finally, develop a strategic plan that integrates the findings from the capability assessments into a cohesive maturity-building roadmap. Focus on building the change maturity level of the CMO, as this will directly influence change initiatives and organizational agility. The other capabilities—such as IT governance, project management, and leadership maturity—should inform ongoing projects and transformation efforts that will rely on strong change management.

Assessment Approach:

1. Define the Capability: Begin by defining the specific capability being assessed (e.g., leadership maturity, process maturity, governance).

2. Define the As-Is Situation and Scope: Clearly outline the current state of the capability and determine the scope of the assessment.

3. Conduct the Assessment: Use methods such as interviews, workshops, surveys, and desk research to collect relevant data. This should involve key stakeholders and subject-matter experts within the organization.

4. Process the Data: Organize the collected information into structured sections, separating the factual data, insights, and advisory recommendations. This clarity ensures that anyone reviewing the assessment can easily understand the outcomes.

5. Conduct a Handover Session: Present the findings to relevant stakeholders and key leadership. This session allows for feedback and helps decision-makers understand how the assessment informs their future work.

6. Integrate Outcomes into Planning: Finally, incorporate the assessment outcomes into the organization's strategic planning, roadmaps, and next steps. This ensures the insights gained from the assessment directly influence organizational strategy and future initiatives.

Strategies for Developing Organizational Change Maturity

Developing organizational change maturity requires a systematic approach that goes beyond focusing on the CMO. The following strategies can help shift the focus from just managing change to building long-term change capabilities:

- **Think Big, Start Small:** Start by focusing on small, high-impact areas where change management can deliver quick wins. This could involve creating a Change Playbook for high-stakes projects such as mergers & acquisitions (M&A) or digital transformations, where effective change management is critical to success. Over time, expand these capabilities across the organization.

- **Democratize Change:** One of the key aspects of building organizational change maturity is democratizing change management so that it becomes a core competency of all employees, not just a small group of change managers. The CMO can help achieve this by developing toolkits, running training sessions, and providing advisory services to equip all employees with basic change management skills. This reduces reliance on the CMO for every project and helps embed change capabilities across the organization.

- **Align with Strategic Goals:** For change maturity to be sustainable, it must be aligned with the organization's strategic objectives. The CMO should map change initiatives to the organization's long-term goals and work to ensure that value creation—whether through increased efficiency, innovation, or risk management—is measured and communicated.

- **Use a Flexible Framework:** Rigid governance structures can stifle change. Instead, organizations should adopt flexible frameworks that allow for agility in the face of change. The CMO can promote a system where continuous improvement is part of the operating model, ensuring that changes are evaluated, lessons learned are documented, and improvements are made continuously.

- **Assess and Address Organizational Debt:** Organizational debt refers to the accumulated inefficiencies that build up when outdated processes, systems, or structures are left in place. Identifying and addressing this debt is key to increasing organizational agility. The CMO can play a role in assessing organizational debt and helping the business restructure itself in a way that supports smoother, more efficient change.

Organisational Debt and the minus Zero effect

Organizational debt represents a significant barrier to organizational change maturity, and in the C+MMF Organizational Change Maturity Framework, it is viewed as a minus level on the maturity scale. This debt can manifest in outdated structures, obsolete processes, and legacy roles that no longer serve the organization's strategic goals. The key challenge is that organizational debt consumes valuable resources—time, money, and attention—that could otherwise be directed toward maturity-building initiatives. When resources are tied up in maintaining inefficient systems, they hinder an organization's ability to adapt to change and prevent investments in initiatives that could boost change maturity.

In the journey toward organizational change maturity, one of the ultimate goals is to create a lean and agile organization, free from wasteful functions and outdated practices. A truly mature organization is designed to operate efficiently, continuously evolving its processes, structures, and culture. This includes governance models and operating systems, which should be treated as living constructs that adapt in response to internal and external pressures. However, organizational debt works against this objective, creating inertia that limits an organization's flexibility and responsiveness to change.

For many organizations, addressing organizational debt can be a far more transformative action than making the leap from level 3 to level 4 on the maturity scale. This is because eliminating organizational debt frees up capital, resources, and management attention, which can be reinvested into strategic projects that foster change maturity. Additionally, removing unnecessary processes and structures enhances operational agility, allowing the organization to respond quickly to market shifts, emerging technologies, and new customer demands. In this sense, tackling organizational debt can have an immediate impact on ROI and deliver significant value, sometimes exceeding the incremental gains of traditional maturity-building initiatives.

Moreover, organizations burdened by debt often find that their ability to innovate and adapt is severely restricted. The outdated systems and cultural norms that contribute to debt act as barriers to fostering a forward-thinking and change-capable culture. Without addressing these core issues, any attempt to build change maturity risks being short-lived or ineffective. To achieve sustainable growth in change maturity, organizations must prioritize identifying and eliminating organizational debt, viewing it as a prerequisite for long-term success in the fast-paced, ever-evolving business landscape.

Case Study: Developing Organizational Change Capability in an IT Consultancy Organization

An IT consultancy firm, specializing in digital transformation and enterprise solutions, faced significant technical debt and governance debt, severely impacting operational efficiency, agility, and service delivery. The organization decided to enhance its organizational change capability using the C+MMF model, a framework that maps key organizational capabilities alongside change capability levels. This assessment provided a strategic foundation to address deficiencies and drive long-term transformation while also be the foundation for establishing the first foundations of a CMO.

The first action taken was mapping Key Capabilities and Identifying Debt. Using the C+MMF model, the organization conducted a thorough assessment of its technical and governance maturity levels. The findings revealed that technical and organisational debt where key areas of attention and funding for the organisation to be able to achieve its goals.

The assessment highlighted that without addressing these debt areas, change capability would remain stagnant, preventing the firm from achieving business agility and operational excellence which were the two leading value propositions for the organisation in 2023.

After an initial assessment phase, there were three tracks taken. Two focusing on the outcomes of the assessment and the third track had the goal of capturing anything that would form the founding change capability which could include strategy, tools and assets. The three tracks were:

1. Technical Debt: Legacy systems, fragmented IT infrastructure, and numerous shadow applications were reducing efficiency and complicating service delivery.
2. Governance Debt: The governance structure was outdated, heavy on redundant protocols, and lacked effective job architecture, impacting employee engagement and accountability.
3. Building change capability which also included supporting the creation of strategy, managing stakeholders at program level.

Track 1: Eliminating Technical Debt through IT Capability Mapping and Strategic Roadmap Development

Actions Taken:

- **Conducted a technology maturity assessment to clarify:**
  - Areas where investment would yield the highest impact.
  - Areas requiring immediate intervention to reduce technical debt.

- **Developed a strategic IT roadmap focusing on:**
  - Technology consolidation: Choosing a single platform technology (Microsoft) to unify operations.
  - Eliminating IT complexity: Removing unnecessary shadow apps and point solutions.
  - Enhancing agility and governance alignment: Creating IT structures that support streamlined decision-making and automated compliance processes.

- Initiated first technical debt streamlining initiatives from the roadmap and simplification of the IT landscape within the organisation. This was set up as a program of projects that represented different initiatives. Strategic change management was carried out on the program level, while each project received attention for stakeholder management and training.

- **Change Capability Development:**
  - Trained employees with role-specific change capability training, enabling them to manage small and medium-scale change activities independently.

- Reinforced training after implementing new technology updates, ensuring better adoption and sustained improvement in customer engagement.

2. Addressing Governance Debt: Job Architecture and Process Maturity Assessment

Actions Taken:

- **Conducted a governance maturity and job architecture assessment, revealing:**
  - Inconsistent job architecture, causing role confusion and disengagement.
  - Redundant governance processes, leading to inefficiencies and unnecessary compliance checks.
- Implemented updated job architecture, aligning employee responsibilities with business objectives.
- Revised governance models, integrating them into a new IT-regulated system with automated updates.
- **Change Capability Development:**
  - Designed targeted training for underperforming role areas.
  - Implemented governance alignment from onboarding to career development, ensuring long-term clarity and accountability.
  - Introduced automated governance structures, reducing manual monitoring.

Outcome After One Year:

- One-third of the strategic IT roadmap completed, achieving a Level One maturity in technology capabilities.
- Elimination of significant technical debt, improving operational agility while cutting costs of maintenance.
- Improved process efficiency, accelerating customer service and internal workflows. Customer onboarding capacity increased by 400%, without expanding the workforce.

- Reduction of redundant applications, simplifying workflows and cutting costs of multiple overlapping applications.
- Employees trained in change capability, improving adaptation and system integration.

By leveraging the C+MMF model, this IT consultancy successfully eliminated technical and governance debt, built stronger change capability, and significantly improved organizational agility. Their structured approach, combining technology, governance, and process improvements, resulted in measurable efficiency gains and long-term sustainability. This case study highlights the importance of aligning technical investments with organizational change strategies, ensuring continuous improvement and resilience in an ever-evolving business landscape.

Chapter Conclusion:

In this chapter we looked at how organisational change maturity relies on both key organisational capabilities like project management and change capability. The C+MMF framework integrates all capabilities systemically and provides a tool for comparison as well as strategic decision making to increase value outcomes from limited resources. This is just one tool in a kit of essential tools required for truly building organisational change maturity and they are not rocket science to create, the hardest part is establishing the universal recognition and ownership of any new ontology or other tool that might be created.

Building organizational change maturity is essential for ensuring that the organization is adaptable, innovative, and capable of sustaining long-term success. The CMO must focus not only on managing change but also on embedding change capabilities throughout the organization. By using tools like maturity assessments, change playbooks, and flexible frameworks, the CMO can help democratize management of change, ensuring that change becomes an organizational-wide competency rather than a siloed function.

In the next chapter, the theme will be the practical setting up of a CMO. This chapter will focus on the bare bones of a CMO and be the foundation for connecting more of the themes in this book.

References

- Anderson, Dean. *Beyond Change Management: How to Achieve Breakthrough Results through Conscious Change Leadership.* Wiley, 2010.

- Cameron, Esther, and Mike Green. *Making Sense of Change Management: A Complete Guide to the Models, Tools, and Techniques of Organizational Change.* Kogan Page, 2020.

- Doppelt, Bob. *Leading Change Toward Sustainability: A Change-Management Guide for Business, Government, and Civil Society.* Routledge, 2017.

- Hammer, Michael. *The Process Audit: Lessons from the Capability Maturity Model Integration (CMMI).* Harvard Business Review, 2007.

- Kotter, John P. *Accelerate: Building Strategic Agility for a Faster-Moving World.* Harvard Business Review Press, 2014.

- The Change Management Institute. *The Effective Change Manager: The Change Management Body of Knowledge.* Vivid Publishing, 2014.

- Snowden, Dave. "A Leader's Framework for Decision Making." *Harvard Business Review*, 2007, https://hbr.org/2007/11/a-leaders-framework-for-decision-making. Accessed 2 March 2025.

- Prosci. *Change Management Maturity Model*, 2020. www.prosci.com.

- LaMarsh, Daryl. *Change Capability Assessment Model (CCAM).* LaMarsh Global, 2019.

- Greenleaf, Robert. *Servant Leadership: A Journey into the Nature of Legitimate Power and Greatness.* Paulist Press, 1977.

- Bass, Bernard M., and Ronald E. Riggio. *Transformational Leadership.* Lawrence Erlbaum Associates, 2006.

- Kanikani, Isolde. *Change Management During Unprecedented Times.* IGI Global, 2022. www.igi-global.com/book/change-management-during-unprecedented-times/308290.

- COBIT Framework for Governance and Management of Enterprise IT. ISACA, 2019.

- Barnett, Gordon. "Organization Design Capability Maturity Drives Transformation Success." *Forrester*, November 2019, https://www.forrester.com/blogs/organization-design-capability-maturity-drives-transformation-success/
- BCG. "Change Management Delta model." *BCG*, 2012, https://www.bcg.com/publications/2012/change-management-post-merger-integration-changing-change-management.
- Turetken, Oktay, and Amy Van Looy. *Capability and Maturity Models in Business Process Management*. Edward Elgar Publishing, 2024.
- Van Looy, Amy. *Business Process Maturity: A Comparative Study on a Sample of Business Processes*. Springer, 2014.
- Wageman, Ruth. *Senior Leadership Teams: What It Takes to Make Them Great*. Harvard Business Review Press, 2008.

Chapter 6

Setting Up a Change Management Office

While many organizations focus solely on building change management capability—relying on a small team to handle change initiatives—this often leads to limited scalability and a disconnect from strategic goals. A successful CMO must aim to democratize change capability across the organization, fostering change maturity where employees at all levels and in all roles can manage role related change effectively. Leaving a clear space for dedicated SMEs to tackle the complex change and continue to provide support to change capability growth int he organisation.

Establishing a Change Management Office (CMO) is a critical step toward building organizational change maturity and this chapter focuses on the practical steps for a straight forward CMO setup. This chapter also brings together all the information shared in previous chapters together, and will act as a foundation for the ones to come.

Key Steps in Establishing a CMO

The process of setting up a CMO begins with a clear vision and understanding of what the CMO will accomplish in and for the organisation. This starts with defining its purpose, which should go beyond operational support for individual projects. The CMO's objective must be aligned with building organizational change maturity, ensuring that change becomes an integral part of the organization's culture, governance, and day-to-day activities. This vision should outline how the CMO will help achieve strategic business goals and deliver measurable value, both in the short and long term.

Step-by-Step Setup Guide:

1. **Define the Vision, Objectives and scope of a new CMO in relation to the organisations**: The first step in setting up a CMO is to define a clear vision and set of objectives. This includes articulating the CMO's role in supporting the organization's

strategy, its expected outcomes, and how it will build change maturity. It is important to frame these objectives in terms of measurable results, such as increased ROI, improved operational efficiency, or enhanced employee engagement.

2. **Create a strategic business case:** A well-crafted strategic business case should be presented to the leadership team, highlighting how the CMO will enhance organizational effectiveness, reduce project failure rates, and ensure alignment with strategic goals.

3. **Secure Executive Sponsorship and funding:** It is vital to secure executive sponsorship from key senior leaders, such as the CEO or CSO. This sponsorship provides the CMO with the necessary authority, resources, and visibility to succeed. It can be helpful to map and analyse the sponsor landscape, particularly where the organisation is complex and has a large number of employees.

4. **Assess value creation through change capability management:** Assessing the areas of value generation through management of change helps the CMO focus efforts where it counts. There is a tendency for trying for 100% coverage when this is practically impossible due to limited resources. Furthermore, releasing value while building change capability ensures a cumulative ROI as well as a one-time ROI.

5. **Assess the building of organisational change capability requirements:** Checking which strategies and outcomes will specifically be of importance to the organisation. Scoping activities will help drive value and make sure the CMO outcomes remain relevant. This can include specific types of change rollout like M&A or digital transformation, compliance in certain ISO standards or requirements for reporting capabilities like the ones needed to comply with the CSDR.

6. **Map the partnership landscape:** The CMO never acts in isolation and will always seek to collaborate with other departments managing change and well as enable change capability in all areas of the business. Mapping out the key integration partners like the TO, PMO, global communications and other directly impacting departments will help see the gap the CMO will fill and the freedom it will have to fill out. Besides this, it can be

interesting to consider other assessments like department or BU change maturity which will help with further strategies.

7. **Design the governance, operating setup and integration Structure:** The internal organizational structure of the CMO needs to be designed, detailing essential roles and responsibilities within the CMO team. Common roles include a Chief Change Officer (CCO), change managers, data analysts, training specialists, and communications experts. Ensuring the reporting lines and operating structures are clear and integrated with other departments, like the PMO or Transformation Office, is also essential for avoiding overlaps in governance. Besides this, the setup of charters can be a great way to align with partners.

8. **Develop the strategic business plan:** A comprehensive strategic business plan is a great way to translate the strategic business case into an executable plan. This should go further than the outlined costs, benefits, and risks associated with creating the office and show how the CMO will grow and tangibly deliver results.

9. **Create the yearly business plan:** While the strategic business plan shows the growth strategy and longer-term vision, the yearly business plan aligns with budgeting and specific goals set on a monthly, quarterly or yearly basis. This document is the short-term guide for getting things done, where goals are closely associated with budget and resourcing.

10. **Setup success criteria, KPIs and baseline for monitoring:** Form the basis of success criteria which can be represented as OKRs or another measurable goal structure appropriate to the organisation. Creating a baseline for monitoring before any actions have been taken, ensures that all progress can be captured. This is vital for showing return on investment and how the CMO delivers value to the organisation. Think on data that will show value realisation on the strategic level, the initiative level, change maturity development and technology adoption. Be mindful that we don't want to monitor activities, but should focus on outcomes and impact.

11. **Build the CMO Team and processes:** Recruit individuals with the required skills and experience in change management and besides this already begin the development of a change cham-

pion network. Training and development opportunities should be provided to ensure that the CMO team is equipped to handle the diverse challenges of organizational change. Alongside this, creation of standardized processes and tools need to be developed to support change initiatives. This could include change playbooks, toolkits for champions to cater for basic change, templates for stakeholder engagement, and KPIs to measure success. Creation of a CMO principles, processes and procedures book is a great way to streamline the onboarding process for new team members and delegate key responsibility areas to grow feeling of ownership and stop bottlenecks so the CMO lead can focus on next steps and strategy.

12. **Develop Tools, automate and facilitate repeat tasks:** Automating and streamlining the work of the extended team from the start is a vital element in building for scalability.

13. **Implement, Monitor, and Adjust:** After the CMO is launched, it is critical to continuously monitor its performance. Metrics and KPIs should track the effectiveness of change initiatives, ensuring that they are delivering value. Regular reviews should also be conducted to adjust strategies based on feedback and evolving business needs. Developing an internal awareness communications plan is vital for growing recognition of the role the CMO plays in the organisation, how employees can engage with it and promoting successful outcomes which support further budgets and growth.

14. **Setup first initiatives for the CMO:** It's important to choose initiatives wisely and prioritise based on sharing quick wins and success stories on a regular basis to grow reputation and trust. A second track of initiatives that develop scalability of the CMO offering is also important, so that profounds steps are made to key strategies like democratising change capability or ChangeOps that will cumulatively and scalably created value over time.

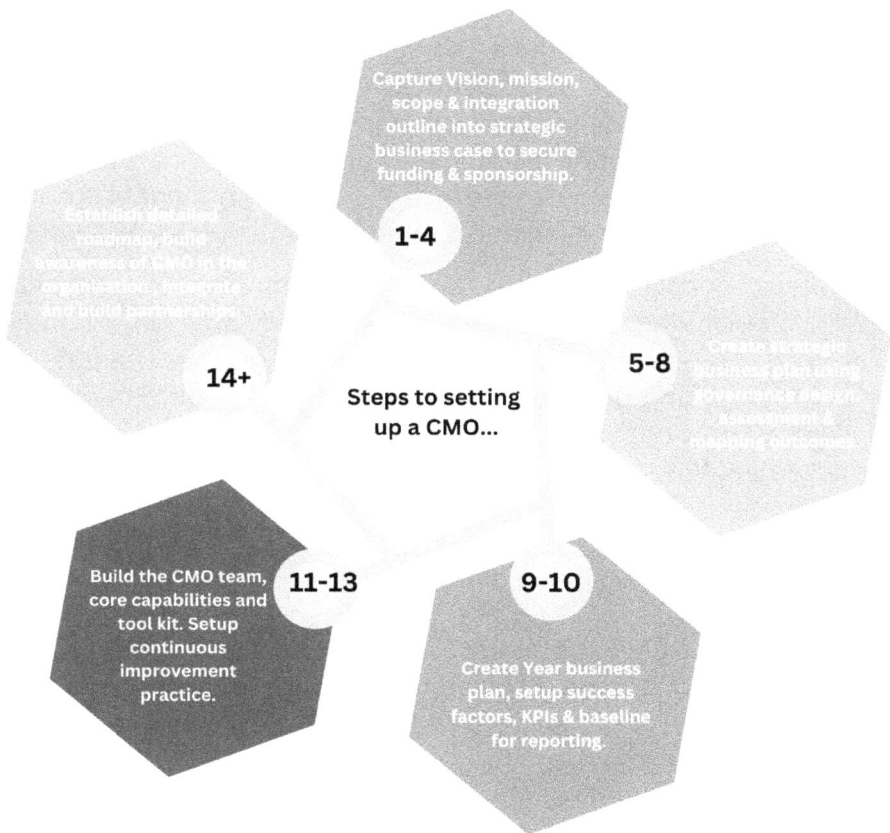

Figure 10: The image above shows the steps in this section. They have been grouped into five areas that is a natural grouping of the activities based on getting them efficiently carried out and in place. These steps focus on the bare bone's setup of a CMO, which can be augmented by further topics and actions discussed in chapters following this one.

Defining and Redefining Strategic Success for CMOs

A crucial aspect of setting up a CMO for long-term strategic success is clearly defining its scope. This means determining not only what the CMO will be responsible for but also setting boundaries to prevent it from becoming overwhelmed or diluted.

One of the first decisions is whether the CMO will focus primarily on change management maturity—which is the ability to manage change within a narrow, project-based context—or on organizational change maturity, which is about fostering change agility across the entire organization. The latter is more strategic and involves embedding change capabilities into every level of the organization, ensuring that employees are equipped to manage change, regardless of the project or initiative.

A related concept is ChangeOps, which emphasizes operationalizing change management practices across the organization. ChangeOps aims to build repeatable, scalable change processes that integrate seamlessly with ongoing business operations, making change management an ongoing part of the organization's culture rather than a temporary, project-based function.

Essential Roles, Responsibilities, and Capabilities within a CMO

A well-functioning CMO requires a competent team with diverse skills and a clear understanding of their roles. The below roles are a representation of those that could be present in a CMO rather than what should always be present. The types of roles required will always depend on the goals of the CMO and the other partners in the organisation.

These roles could include:
- **Chief Change Officer (CCO)**: Oversees the CMO and ensures its alignment with strategic goals. Responsible for engaging stakeholders, advocating for change, and leading high-level change initiatives.
- **Organisational change managers:** Lead change capability and strategic enablement initiatives, coach leaders and carry out organisational level development.
- **Project Change Managers:** Lead individual projects, manage stakeholders, address resistance, and communicate effectively throughout the change process.
- **Program and project managers**: Lead the programs and projects associated with CMO goals and activities.

- **Change Analysts:** Collect and analyse data, provide insights on change initiatives, and track KPIs to ensure that change efforts are on track.
- **Training and Development Specialists:** Design and deliver training programs aimed at enhancing the organization's change management capabilities.
- **Transformation managers:** Lead large scale transformations, usually if the CMO has a TO function or where the organisation is going through a lot of digital change.
- **Technology adoption specialists:** Lead the change and adoption activities on technology rollouts, have specialist knowledge where a specific technology is concerned.
- **Communications Specialists:** Manage internal and external communications to ensure clarity and consistency throughout the change process.
- **Continuous improvement specialists:** Manage transitions of project outcomes into continuous improvement and Center of Excellence that maintains key capabilities driving change on the iterative level. Capabilities could include lean, six sigma, quality management and service performance and excellence expertise.
- **Organisation specific specialists:** Specialist knowledge might be needed by the CMO team to properly integrate expert level knowledge, usually because the organisations products and services require a high level of compliance or industry specific knowledge.

Building the CMO team is not a one-time effort. Continuous professional development and team collaboration are necessary to ensure that the CMO adapts and grows with the organization's needs. Besides this, as the organisation develops so to must the strategy of the CMO which can require other roles or new specialisms. As the CMO and the organisation develop in their respective change maturities, so too will the roles needed to sustain and further develop in line with evolving goals.

Capabilities within a CMO

The CMO goals and scope are important things to define when looking to understand the capabilities that should be built into the CMO team. Broad scoped CMOs that are aligned to organisational change maturity building will need more capabilities to manage the different types of organisational change and maybe some SMEs in key areas too. Defined or small scope CMOs on the other hand have a much more target approach to managing change. Capabilities with a defined scope will be dependent on the targeted area e.g. if the target is to build M&A ROI then strategic OCM consultants working together with SMEs in M&A and finance will be required. If the target area is digital transformation, then there will be a good amount of technical knowledge and capability required to be successful.

Both scopes can be combined into a hybrid approach which is where the think big and start pragmatical approach is advised. This requires the creation of a blueprint for building organisational change capability (broad scope goal) that guides the pragmatic and targeted change initiatives. This way the start pragmatic part of hybrid is still building change capability, and to be explicit this is different to reactionary ad hoc operational level change management on projects where the CMO is lucky if it will build anything scalable.

The natural integration points of a CMO in the company will also define the necessary capabilities. If there is already an established PMO, transformation office, learning and develop or other similar and overlapping departments, then the capabilities the CMO will need might already be in one of these locations. This is why some of the steps in previous chapters are so important. Capture the information from activities in the first chapters in the strategic business case and plan will mean you have the basis for a streamlined building on the CMO team.

Broad Scope

- **Goal:** strategically manage all types of change within the organisation, develop organisational change capability.
- **Key Strategies:** Change-as-a-service, Democratising change, Change Playbooks, CoE
- **Sponsor type:** CEO, CSO (Strategy), COO
- **Collaboration:** Coordinate different OU's managing specific types of change
- **Team capability:** Strategic Organisational change & key organisational capability SME's

Hybrid

Think Big, start pragmatic strategy

Defined Scope

- **Goal:** Realise value from managing change in key and strategically targeted areas of the organisation.
- **Key Strategies:** Value Mapping & Playbooks
- **Sponsor type:** Dependent on the focus area e.g. HR transformation would be the CHRO, Finance transformation would be the CFO.
- **Collaboration:** Focus is on a particular part of the organisation with a centralised effort that connects in relevant parties to realise the intended outcomes.
- **Team capability:** Tactical and operational change management capability based on programs and projects setup. Specialist knowledge in the targeted areas is a plus but not long term viable due to the degree of defined scope and number of changes to different value realising parts of the organisation.

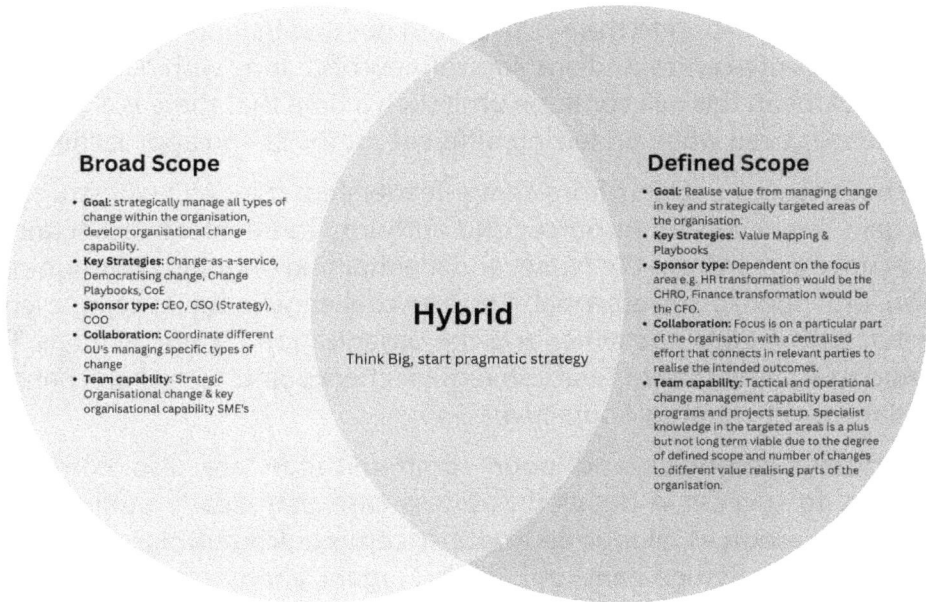

Scoping CMO Integration Approaches

Figure 11: Show three types of scope that will impact the capabilities required by a CMO to be successful. Couple this with having clarity on governance and natural integration partners, one can quickly come to a conclusion about which capabilities are required.

Common Pitfalls and How to Avoid Them

One of the most common pitfalls in setting up a CMO is the lack of executive support placed side by side with a general lack of understanding about the benefits managing change can bring. For some change management is vague and misunderstood, while for others there is confusion about what a CMO might do differently to a HR, Communications, a transformation office or project management office. In part this is due to there being no globally accepted standard to date, and in part it is a natural outward representation of a profession still in its baby shoes and to-date underfunded.

There are common misconceptions along the lines of 'everyone can do change management' to 'thinking it's a model', 'or theoretical without practical application' to the worse case in not understanding what it is at all. The lack of a centralised ontological view of change within the profession will mean this will continue until such a time that there is a general consensus even while preferring different methods and approaches.

Without strong backing from senior leadership, the CMO will struggle to gain the necessary resources and authority to be effective. Securing executive buy-in from the outset and maintaining ongoing communication with sponsors is essential. Another challenge is the misalignment between the CMO's activities and the organization's strategic goals. To avoid this, it is critical to establish regular checkpoints to realign change initiatives with strategic objectives.

Insufficient resources and poor communication are also common barriers to success. A detailed business case that clearly outlines the required resources, alongside a robust communication plan, can help address these issues early on. Finally, organizations often underestimate the importance of standardized processes and tools. Developing a clear framework for how change will be managed across projects helps ensure consistency and effectiveness.

A CMO can directly and indirectly address these pitfalls with the practices shared in this book. While indirectly we can already make a huge shift in perception, there is still a call for direct awareness building of what managing change looks like and the tangible benefits it will achieve.

Case Studies: Successful CMO Implementations

Case Study 1: Global Technology Company

A global technology company established a CMO to support its digital transformation efforts. By securing executive sponsorship in the form of the CIO and developing a business case focused on aligning the CMO's activities with the company's long-term strategy, the CMO was able to implement standardized change processes across multiple regions. The CMO was instrumental in integrating new technologies and optimizing workflows, leading to increased customer satisfaction and operational efficiency.

On the strategic level, the CMO's value generating service to the business was primarily supporting the CIO to further integrate the IT organisation as the beating heart of the business.

Case Study 2: Establishing a CMO in a Healthcare Organization

A leading healthcare group, managing multiple hospitals, clinics, and pharmacies, recognized the urgent need for structured change management to support its long-term strategic objectives. With a centralized decision-making structure and well-established Centers of Excellence (CoEs) for various functions, including a PMO and Transformation Office, the organization sought to integrate a Change Management Office (CMO) to enhance organizational change capability while ensuring alignment with ongoing transformation efforts.

This CMO was designed to operate under a hybrid scope, balancing enterprise-wide change capability development with targeted support for high-impact initiatives and specifically increasing ROI from mergers. The group had two tiers to work on and a decentralised decision-making setup where individual companies had almost full autonomy to adopt global practices or not. This structure greatly impacted the approach to digital transformation and in some places the M&A activity when the bought companies value capability needed to be integrated into existing group companies. Specifically, two critical transformation tracks were identified with change capability building being the underpinning third. See below for how we organised each track including the challenges, strategy and outcomes.

Digital Transformation:
The need to update the operating landscape by centralizing data, adopting new digital health technologies, and modernizing patient care workflows. Hospitals within the group still relied heavily on paper archives dating back to 1960, requiring a structured digitalization strategy.

1. Hospitals relied on paper-based patient records dating back to 1960, leading to inefficiencies, compliance risks, and data security concerns.

2. There was no standardized digital platform across the hospital

111

group, leading to fragmented patient data and operational inconsistencies.

3. Adoption of new digital tools had historically been slow and inconsistent among hospital staff.
4. Updated IT Governance & Security Compliance: Ensured that data privacy, cybersecurity measures, and regulatory requirements were embedded in the new platform.

1. **Strategic Approach:**
   a. Developed a Digital Transformation Change Playbook to standardize digital adoption processes, best practices, and engagement strategies.
   b. Stakeholder Mapping and Engagement Strategy: Identified key clinical, IT, and administrative stakeholders to drive early adoption and feedback loops.
2. **Phased Rollout Approach:**
   a. Phase 1: Pilot implementation in two major hospitals, testing electronic health records (EHR) systems, AI-driven diagnostics, and telemedicine.
   b. Phase 2: Train-the-trainer programs to empower internal champions who would lead the rollout in remaining hospitals, clinics, and pharmacies.
   c. Phase 3: Enterprise-wide deployment, real-time monitoring, and continuous feedback for system refinements.
3. **Outcome-Driven Metrics:**
   a. 50% reduction in administrative time spent on patient records.
   b. Faster and more accurate diagnostics with AI-enabled tools.
   c. Improved regulatory compliance with digital record-keeping and security protocols.

Mergers & Acquisitions (M&A): With an inorganic growth strategy, the organization frequently acquired new hospitals, clinics, and pharmacies. To maximize post-merger value, a structured M&A change playbook was needed to harmonize processes, protocols, and technology systems across all facilities, ensuring consistency in patient care delivery.

1. Post-merger integrations lacked consistent processes, leading to delayed synergies, cultural misalignment, and operational inefficiencies.
2. Each acquired hospital, clinic, or pharmacy used different protocols, IT systems, and patient care workflows.
3. Limited standardization led to higher operational costs, compliance risks, and patient experience inconsistencies.

1. **Strategic Approach:**
   a. **Developed an M&A Change Playbook Scenario** to create a structured integration model for new acquisitions.
2. **Focus Areas:**
   a. Governance Standardization: Aligned all acquired hospitals with the group's policies, compliance requirements, and governance framework.
   b. Technology Integration: Ensured that new entities adopted the centralized IT platform, EHR system, and cybersecurity protocols.
   c. Process & Protocol Harmonization: Mapped critical clinical, administrative, and operational processes across entities, defining a standard operating model.
   d. Cultural & Workforce Integration: Implemented onboarding and training programs for employees from acquired hospitals to align with the group's patient care philosophy and practices.
3. **Outcome-Driven Metrics:**
   a. Faster time-to-value realization post-acquisition, reducing integration timelines from 12 months to 6 months.
   b. Increased operational efficiency by reducing redundant administrative processes.
   c. Enhanced patient safety and care standardization across all hospitals in the group.

Change capability building: CMO Setup and Organizational Integration

- **Sponsorship and Business Case Development:** Given the scale of transformation required, the Chief Strategy Officer (CSO) sponsored the CMO initiative, advocating for strategic funding at the C-level. A business case outlined the need for a formalized change capability, quantifying potential ROI from reduced inefficiencies, improved patient care outcomes, and regulatory compliance enhancements. Once funding was granted, the CMO was formally structured as a CoE, closely collaborating with the existing PMO and Transformation Office to ensure that change management efforts were deeply integrated into enterprise-wide projects and programs.

- **Building the CMO Team and Governance Model:** The CMO team was carefully structured to balance both broad change capability-building efforts and targeted transformation projects:
    - i   Two Senior Strategic Change Managers: Focused on designing enterprise-wide change frameworks, training programs, and methodologies for building organizational change maturity.
    - Technology Adoption Specialist (SME): Dedicated to supporting the implementation of the new digital health platform, ensuring smooth adoption across clinical and administrative functions.
    - Project Manager: Responsible for managing CMO-related projects, timelines, and stakeholder alignment within the hospital group.
    - Planned Continuous Improvement Manager: This role, set to be filled in the next phase, would oversee the transition from project-based change efforts to ongoing continuous improvement and quality management, ensuring long-term sustainability.
    - Planned Strategic Organizational Change Manager (OCM): A high-level change expert with 10+ years of experience would be brought in at the beginning of the next major M&A project. This person would take ownership of the M&A change playbook scenario, ensuring seamless post-merger integration and cultural alignment across acquired entities.

Key Results & Business Impact

1. **Stronger Organizational Change Capability:** The new CMO enabled the hospital group to transition from ad-hoc change

management to a structured, scalable, and strategic change approach.

2. **Improved Digital Readiness:** Legacy paper-based processes were phased out, with hospitals shifting to real-time digital records.

3. **Faster M&A Integrations:** Post-merger harmonization time was cut in half, significantly accelerating the realization of synergies.

4. **Higher Employee Engagement and Adoption:** Change adoption programs empowered hospital staff, IT teams, and administrators, reducing resistance to digital and process changes.

5. **Long-Term Sustainability:** The integration of continuous improvement frameworks ensured that change management efforts extended beyond project-based implementations, fostering a culture of adaptability.

This case study highlights the critical role of a well-structured CMO in supporting large-scale transformations within a centralized healthcare organization. By balancing broad change capability development with targeted, scenario-driven change playbooks, the CMO was able to drive strategic digital transformation, support M&A activities, and future-proof the organization for continued growth.

With governance integration, strategic technology adoption, and employee engagement at its core, this hybrid CMO model ensured long-term value realization for the hospital group. Looking forward, continued refinement of change methodologies, investment in AI-driven change analytics, and a focus on sustaining organizational agility will be key to scaling its impact.

Chapter Conclusion:

In this chapter we looked at how to practically setup a CMO and the scope strategies one could use to further build the CMO team. Setting up a Change Management Office is a strategic endeavour that requires careful planning, alignment with organizational goals, and strong leadership support. But at the same time a pragmatic approach to getting the CMO setup is vital. Thinking along the lines of a think big, start proactive is a great way to go. If we are too perfectionist we won't get started and likewise if we start without a framework guide growth, we risk wasting a lot of time on double or rework. A framework or blueprint helps to align smaller initiatives to a bigger strategic picture, where every effort counts towards building scaled change and value for the organisation.

By following these steps and avoiding common pitfalls, organizations can establish a CMO that drives both immediate and long-term value. More importantly, a well-designed CMO will focus not just on operational support but on the scalable building of organizational change maturity, embedding change capability across the workforce and ensuring that the organization remains agile, competitive, and capable of continuous improvement.

In the next chapter, the theme will be about defining the strategic capability of the CMO itself. While earlier chapters looked at CMO alignment to the business vision and strategy, the next one will focus on the internal strategies and alignment required for success. In the end both the organisations strategy and that of the CMO need to systemically align, with the CMO directly feeding into the organisational level strategy.

References

- OCM Solution. "Best 2024 Guide to Establish and Manage a Change Management CoE Read more at OCM Solution: https://www.ocmsolution.com/change-management-coe-guide/." *OCM Solution*, 2000, https://www.ocmsolution.com/change-management-coe-guide/.
- Ottavi, Leslie. "PMO, CMO and TMO: what they are and how they drive change agility." *iTalent Digital*, 14 July 2023, https://info.italentdigital.com/blog/pmo-cmo-and-tmo-what-they-are-and-how-they-align-to-drive-change-agility.
- Franklin, Melanie. "Change Management Office – Benefits and Structure." 2018, https://agilechangemanagement.co.uk/wp-content/uploads/2018/08/CMO-whitepaper-FINAL.pdf.
- Marsicano, Vincent. *The Change Management Office (CMO). The Change Diaries*, 18 Oct. 2022.
- Paton, Robert A., and James McCalman. *Change Management: A Guide to Effective Implementation*. Sage, 2016.
- Proclipse Consulting. *How to Set Up a Change Management Office: A Practical Guide*. Proclipse, 2021.
- Wipro Consulting. *How a Change Management Office Can Solve the CIO's ROI Problems*. Wipro, 2022.
- Kanikani, Isolde. *Change Management During Unprecedented Times*. IGI Global, 2022.
- LaMarsh, Daryl. *Change Capability Assessment Model (CCAM)*. LaMarsh Global, 2019.
- Creasey, Tim. *The Change Management Office: What It Is and Why Your Organization Needs One*. Prosci, 2020.
- CMMI Institute. "Capability Maturity Model Integration." www.cmmiinstitute.com.

Chapter 7

Ensuring the Strategic Success of the CMO

After the initial foundations of a CMO are setup, there are a number of different strategies that can be incorporated into both the goals, integration and operating strategies. It is important to consider the organisations change needs when it comes to choosing and prioritising strategies in this chapter but also keep in mind that this chapter is focused on the strategy of the CMO. While this should align to realising value and organisation goals, there is more definition needed around how the CMO will reach critical stability, scale and work with the given change needs of the organisation.

In this chapter, overall strategic success factors will be covered together with a deep dive into some of the key strategies that can be used as part of the CMO development.

Defining Strategic Success for CMOs

Strategic success for a Change Management Office (CMO) is not just about facilitating the execution of individual change initiatives. It is about embedding change management into the very fabric of the organization so that it becomes part of the organization's DNA. To achieve this, the CMO must align itself with broader business objectives and become a critical function that contributes to long-term value and success. At the same time, the CMO must have its own strategy for realising goals once they have been cascaded down and learn to relate this in all partnerships within the organisation.

There are several key dimensions to defining strategic success for a CMO:

- **Alignment with Organizational Strategic Goals:** The CMO's activities should be directly tied to the organization's mission and strategic objectives. Whether the business goal is to enhance customer satisfaction, improve operational efficiency, or drive innovation, the CMO must ensure that its change

118

initiatives support these goals. This requires deep involvement in strategic planning, ensuring that change management is not just a function that reacts to projects but a proactive driver of the organization's long-term vision. Scope and mandate to deliver on goals is vital. These can be created through goals aligned with goal frameworks, operating models and governance.

- **Delivering High-Impact Change Initiatives**: The ability to deliver successful change initiatives that meet deadlines, stay within budget, and realize intended outcomes is crucial. Success isn't only measured by project completion but by the quality and sustainability of the results. With limited budget and resources, it's important to make sure that the CMO doesn't get pulled into operational level activities or the temptation to try to put change management on every project. Instead search for where high returns of value can be realised through management of change and where success stories can be actively created to promote the CMO as a successful entity.

- **Stakeholder Engagement and Satisfaction:** Success can also be measured by how well the CMO engages with its stakeholders—executives, employees, and customers—and by the degree of satisfaction stakeholders feel with the change processes and outcomes. Stakeholder buy-in is essential for continuous momentum and for ensuring the CMO's role is valued. Democratising change as a strategy builds economies of scale and is just one of many ways to engage stakeholders as owners of change rather than being bombarded by it. The success of the CMO depends on having the right talent and team members should not only possess expertise in change management but should also bring skills in data analysis, communication, and project management. This multidisciplinary capability enables the CMO to tackle both the people side of change and the technical aspects required for successful transformation.

- **Scalable delivery of value:** Through the facilitation of change on key initiatives and the growing CoE, a CMO can build organisational change capability with deliberate strategy where the desired maturity level is concerned. Standardized, scalable, and repeatable processes are necessary to ensure consistency and efficiency across change initiatives. Developing playbooks, templates, and frameworks that can be customized for different projects will help ensure that the CMO operates efficiently and effectively. Through democratisation of change capability strategies coupled with a network built around an active Community of Practice (CoP), organisational change capability becomes scalable. To ensure the CMO is continuously delivering value, it's important to establish mechanisms for monitoring and evaluating the success of change initiatives. This involves regularly reviewing performance data, stakeholder feedback, and strategic alignment to make necessary adjustments.

Ultimately, strategic success is about positioning the CMO as a critical enabler of business transformation and long-term agility, not just as a project facilitator.

Deep dive into the strategic tool kit

The following sections will each expand on the four above strategic areas and detail out specific strategies that can be applied to a CMO. They can be mixed and matched depending on the CMO's scope and budget for managing change.

Assessing Organizational Change Maturity

This has already been covered extensively in the previous chapter, but is important to mention as a vital strategy for the CMO. This is based on creating a baseline of organisational change maturity and further information that can drive next steps. The baseline can be used to show progress in talks about how success and how the CMO brings value to the organisation. While we can guess at what might be good for building change capability in organisations, properly assessing the organisations current capability, readiness for development and target areas for development is vital for effectively using limited resources in the right way.

ChangeOps: Harnessing the power of Change in organisations

Implementing ChangeOps is a strategic approach that ensures change management processes are embedded into the operational structure of the organization. This means that the CMO's efforts are not confined to managing change on an ad-hoc, project-by-project basis but are instead built into the day-to-day functioning of the organization.

ChangeOps combines the essence of change and operations into a powerful concept for modern businesses. In recent years, the idea of managed change has gained traction, often linked to projects, programs, portfolios, and organization-wide initiatives. Business operations encompass the daily activities that drive enterprise value and profitability, including governance and structures that ensure the effective delivery of value.

ChangeOps unifies all types of organizational change, from Organizational Change Management (OCM) to project-based and continuous improvement initiatives. It focuses on realizing value by creating a seamless flow of change along the value chain, leveraging value workshops, and integrating both digital and non-digital value propositions.

This strategic approach promotes the development of organizational change maturity over mere change management maturity. It encourages cross-departmental collaboration around change, giving ownership of this vital capability across organisations. It emphasizes using the right type of change to meet strategic needs and aligning business goals with pragmatic outcomes driven by people, processes, technology and data. Democratising change by evolving every individual in our organisations to have at least a basic change capability, building this further based on role-specific and appropriate skill development. Incorporating understandings for systems theory, working with informal networks alongside formal organisation structures to realise a deepened understanding and dual operating system approach. Last but not least, connecting organisations through change maturity built around the already established partnerships and interdependencies existing today.

By adopting a holistic and systemic approach, ChangeOps enhances organizational resilience and capability, ensuring businesses thrive in an ever-evolving landscape.

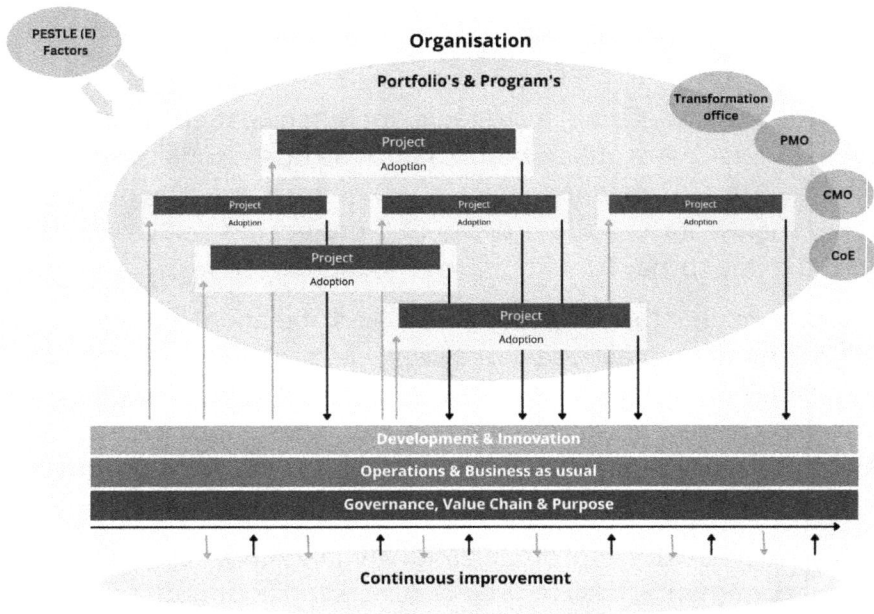

Figure 12: This image brings together many of the key themes talked about throughout this book. It shows the way projects interface with operations and business as usual, the stabilising factors also known as the oscillating platform in ChangeOps and the space for continuous improvement. ChangeOps method asks practitioners to connect different types of change to increase value flows in organisations. A simple example is where project outcomes are embedded into continuous improvement practices to decrease the reliance on projects and next big investment. The CMO would be the natural orchestrator of ChangeOps, including the other units that manage specific aspects of change into partnership.

ChangeOps emphasizes scalability and repeatability. By developing standardized processes, tools, and playbooks that can be applied across various change initiatives, the CMO ensures that change management becomes an ongoing, integrated function. The goal of ChangeOps is to create an agile organization that can rapidly adapt to new challenges and opportunities, reducing the reliance on a central change management team and democratizing change capability across the business.

Democratising Change capability

Democratising change is truly an important strategy that gives a CMO both the opportunity to scale and specifically grows change capability within the organisation. This is not simply about leadership capability where more are busy developing some comprehensive approaches, or about making more change managers. Democratising change is about empowering each and every individual within the organisation, and doing this in a role and experience relevant way.

Change leaders are those who manage change from multiple different contexts, levels of the organisation and using different toolkits to achieve it depending on the types of change they are working with. They are not necessarily established hierarchical positions like the word ´leader´ might suggest. Change champions are a good example of change leaders, where typically influencers and specialists are asked to become part of major change rollouts supporting with communications and training. But there are many more besides. Line managers and capability leaders drive change both in the form of developing individuals within teams, services and goals. C-level drive another type of change that is often longer term and strategic, ensuring that strategy is not just created but executed. In a service delivery organisation consultants, project managers, success advisors and service desk centres are all managing change with customers on a daily basis. So too are internal departments like HR, Communications, Finance and Operations.

Democratising change by building change leaders in every hook of the organisation is not only important to drive organisational change, but it also enables individuals to thrive in these times where change does build up. There is an important mindset shift needed by individuals for this. Ten or more years ago, we might one to two changes we feel as an individual in our organisation at any one time. Coupled with this were different ways of working, tends of thinking and doing that meant other things were prioritised over changeability. Lending a thought from Kaizen, if we can used to changing everything in our environment consistently, we can embrace change as a way of life and the associated learning capability needed to do this. Nowadays we face closer to five or six changes within our working environment which if zooming out from specific initiatives, would culminate in this continually changing environment just mentioned.

So where does the CMO come into all this? As the drive of Change capability, democratising change is one essential program of initiatives to be organised. A practical example of what this can look like is a program containing the following ongoing initiatives cohesively sharing the same change methodology but tailored to roles realising valuable outcomes. The below example is in an IT consulting and implementation organisation where there are internal and external customers.

Program democratising change: Mentioning role specific training related to value outcomes only, by no means an exhaustive list.

- Leadership: individual change capability, strategy execution and driving change within the organisation. For some leadership roles like a CEO, CSO or CRO, there is also an element of driving successful change in the organisation's external environment and translating this in order to help their organisation thrive. These roles can also play a major role in diminishing change fatigue.

- PMO officers: individual change capability, internal customer and project realisation with key change management principles mixed in. Driving value by recognising opportunities that arise from unmanaged or wasteful change.

- Functional consultants delivering to customers: individual change capability, change management skills that support customer engagement and motivation, ways they can apply techniques for supporting learning and behavioural change when delivering on projects. This role is well suited to supporting the adoption of new technology being implemented because they naturally have a deeper level of knowledge about the technology. Train them on complimentary change management skills and you probably have a more effective individual than placing a traditional change manager there.

- Project Managers delivering to customers: This is similar to the functional consultant, but due to the relative differences of role and expertise, complimentary change skills for a project manager are stakeholder mapping and analysis, building out

124

project governance with awareness of the as-is and to-be governance, driving role adoption where new roles have been introduced. Often project managers already have a full plate, so it's good to gage whether they should have a basic change tool kit and have other supporting roles to cater for more within the service design, or make this the go to role for simple and medium complex change. In this example there was a dedicated transformation team to support with the medium and complex change.

- Success advisors delivering to customers: This role is supporting the customer to get the most out of the products or services that have been sold. In this case, there was a high level of stakeholder management and technology adoption skills that would make a huge difference to the value they would bring to customers. Training them on this not only improved the service and customer satisfaction, it also gave a clear tool kit the success advisors could use which was more or less the same as a change manager.

This is just one example, that involved ongoing training after an initial rollout where over two thirds of the company were trained. We maintained and grew the change capability through the following:

- **New joiners onboarding:** This meant anyone new to the company would get the same training as their peers, growing the percentage trained in the organisation. Focus was on basic change capability building and role specific value enablement.

- **Monthly Knowledge sessions:** These provided deep dives into particular topics that were applicable to all roles and introduced new tools and assets they could use within their work. Themes included stakeholder management, motivation and engagement, giving success training and workshops, coaching skills, communication skills to name a few.

- **Community of practice (CoP):** This was setup as a bi monthly townhall with the focus on sharing updates to the CoE (CMO and change capability centre), presented new inspirational themes and topics, and get everyone into practical small group discussions to further explore themes together.

Within one year, we had trained 600 out of 740 people in the company and the number of untrained was quickly diminishing through targeted training to fill any gaps. Soft skills and change capability grew in the company to the extent that we created the change meter. This was a meter or quick assessment anyone in the company could do to see what level of change their initiative would create. For simple gaged projects there was a tool kit made available where anyone receiving the new joiners onboarding, could lead the change and there were on-demands trainings available for particular activities within the available change playbook. Medium complexity changes were still led by individuals but a coach would be made available from the Transformation and OCM team. Complex internal changes involved a Transformation and OCM consultant leading the change supported as much as possible by employees in the company. So, by building change capability directed as improving customer satisfaction, we also with a few basic tools created an internal flexible change capability run by many employees within the company.

Democratising change is, in essence, about enabling every single employee to step into a continuous change mindset where they can successfully become empowered leaders of change in their organisations. This directly goes against the outcomes often seen when a CMO focuses on building change management maturity instead of organisational change capability.

Think big, act pragmatic approach

We tend to either get lost in perfectionism or stuck in reinventing the wheel due to decision making that's too short term. Resulting in a build-up of siloed decisions that when not properly embedded become organisational debt and a major minus on the Change capability maturity scale. This strategy promotes establishing a strategic light framework to guide scalable growth while pragmatically getting value realised on the short term.

With the amount of change we experience currently; any heavily documented approach will get outdated before it's finished and the experience of working with such an approach is often that it slows progress. On the other hand, quick short-term decision making that's focused on the quick win over building for the future quickly builds up a barrier of unintegrated governance, processes and structures (organisation debt) that take time to navigate before change can be implemented. Neither of these are optimal and both inadvertently fight either change or agility.

Instead, setting up a think big framework that's as light as possible while still being a clear guide for rapid growth ensures that we can create clear goals and alignment of multiples parties. This framework also enables involved parties to get proactive and take responsibility to drive key areas for the short and middle terms. When setting up the framework, it's good to keep away from perfectionism and opt instead for the minimum viable product approach, iterating where needed to get the job done.

An example of this strategic approach is nicely fitting in a manufacturing organisation where they are setting up a CoE with the goal of connecting workers across plants via a new technical tool augmented by a community of practice setup. The short-term thinking approach would be to just get started without clarity about what knowledge and capability the organisations needed to capture in order to realise value. This would lead to a quick start, potential success, but also high potential for investing in capabilities that don't bring value. So, a good amount of rework and waste would be involved. The other approach would be too deeply assessed and document the capabilities, the situation and the value the organisation is seeking to achieve with the setup of the CoE. Here the initial exercises would probably result is a ton of information put into a report that will only collect dust and doesn't help to get started.

In this scenario, the think big would be to create a light framework that ensures clear governance, roles and responsibilities together with a set of high priority capabilities to capture and a further list of lower priority ones. The pragmatic steps are done with a learn hard mentality, first delivering on the known capabilities and items that need to be setup and then step into the more investigative mode of assessing the lower priority areas. Importantly the pragmatic steps are focused on realising value and as quickly as possible, but all assets and outcomes are built in line with the framework and build the CoE.

Operate to become obsolete

This strategy aims to focus the CMO the fact that if the CMO does a good job, they will be out of work. The sheer amount of change requires ongoing support and maintenance of a CMO. But making decisions based on what will enable the organisation over the internal focus of improvement activities that might or might not realise value will support a healthy CMO that can meet further goals in this list. This strategy acts as a check mechanism for if the CMO is on the right track with building organisational change capability instead of getting lost in maintaining itself.

Value over 100% coverage of change management:

Prioritize change initiatives based on their potential for delivering high ROI and value to the organization. This ensures that the CMO focuses its limited resources on areas that will have the most significant impact on business outcomes. While in many cases established change management activities deliver value, it's not always the case. Focusing on value might mean thin coverage sometimes but it keeps us true to goals and desired outcomes. This strategy can be as simple as a checking mechanism, where at any given time the CMO team can ask whether what is being worked on is actually the most relevant thing for creating value. Besides this, there is a more involved way to properly focus on value with the support of value mapping.

The interplay between value and change is both inevitable and profound. Value represents the tangible and intangible benefits delivered to customers, stakeholders, and the organization itself. Change, on the other hand, is the mechanism through which this value is created, refined, or delivered. ChangeOps, a strategic approach to managing and aligning the various types of change, emphasizes creating seamless flows of value within organizations. By strategically harnessing change, we align actions with the organization's purpose, driving efficiency and relevance.

To fully appreciate the relationship between value and change, we must understand that while value requires change to materialize, not all change inherently generates value. Mapping value and change can illuminate wasteful activities, uncover opportunities for improvement, and highlight areas ripe for investment. For instance, areas with high levels of change but no structured management often miss opportunities to deliver ROI. Value mapping techniques provide clarity on which changes drive results versus those that detract from strategic objectives.

The different flows of value within an organization—such as operational, strategic, human resource, and transformation flows—can also be viewed as flows of change. These flows can be designed, influenced, and optimized to enhance overall performance. Forming a very practical and holistic framework to work with. Drawing from methodologies like Goldratt's Theory of Constraints and Toyota's Lean principles, we can translate these manufacturing and system-based strategies to any organizational framework, smoothing out the cycles and pathways through which value moves by essentially managing change.

For the change manager who often struggles to make a case for change, establishing this intrinsic relationship between value and change is an extremely important one. Directly tying value realisation into the essence of our work, ensures a healthier and measurable approach that not only delivers ROI as a onetime event for a particular project, but becomes cumulative ROI with the right continuous re-use and improvement measures in place.

Improving value flows benefits organizations in multiple ways. Operational excellence, agility, cost savings, improved employee satisfaction, and faster delivery to customers are just some examples. Recognizing how different flows function—from horizontal operational flows to dual operating systems—allows organizations to tackle inefficiencies systematically. By leveraging tools such as network theory and social network analysis, organizations can influence both formal and informal systems to achieve greater alignment and impact.

Understanding and managing these dimensions can unlock unparalleled organizational success, positioning change not just as a process but as a strategic enabler of value. Let's dive deeper into these concepts to discover how organizations can harness the intrinsic relationship between value and change.

Understanding value and change as dynamic, interdependent forces is essential in modern business. Change is the engine of value realization, but not all changes lead to positive outcomes. Misaligned or unmanaged changes can erode resources and stall progress. Using value mapping techniques, organizations can identify:

1. Value-add changes: Directly contribute to organizational goals, e.g. managed change during a merger, or the development of a product into something of value to a customer.
2. Neutral changes: Necessary but do not add significant value (e.g., compliance adjustments), e.g.
3. Wasteful changes: Consume resources without tangible returns.

For example, areas with high change activity but low results often lack structured change management. Using a structured approach to change management and one focusing on value output rather than heavy on plans and activities will take an organisation a long way.

Dual purposing Goal Frameworks & establish CMO as strategic partner

The frameworks that guide goal setting within the CMO and that integrate it with the organisation are critical to its success. OKRs (Objectives and Key Results) and KPIs are widely used goal-setting methods that provide clarity, focus, and alignment. When properly applied, these frameworks ensure that the CMO is working on high-impact initiatives that drive business value in an aligned and agreed way.

Having awareness of and using goal framework setup can lead to:

- OKRs help align the CMO's goals with the broader organizational strategy, breaking down high-level objectives into specific, measurable, and time-bound results. This allows the CMO to ensure that its efforts directly contribute to organizational success.
- KPIs, on the other hand, provide ongoing visibility into the CMO's performance. By defining specific metrics related to the success of change initiatives (e.g., adoption rates, project timelines, or budget adherence), KPIs help ensure that the CMO remains focused on delivering tangible results.

Besides this basic strategic need, goal framework implementation and improvement projects can be dual purposed for building change capability. An example of this is where an organisation is setting up OKRs as the goal framework of choice. The organisation focuses on getting rid of silos with the strategic alignment of OKRs across departments horizontally as well as alignment to the guiding strategic goals vertically. In this setup, departments can check their OKRs against others where there is a high degree of overlap or potential gaps missed by both parties. If the CMO leads the OKR role out with an additional focus on inter departmental collaboration and understanding, then the CMO is already building on a foundation for more types of projects.

When these frameworks are misaligned with the organization's strategy, or when the CMO's goals are disconnected from business outcomes, the CMO risks losing relevance. This misalignment can lead to wasted resources, missed opportunities, and the perception that the CMO is not delivering value.

Stronger together

The focus here is on collaboration and integration with other organizational units. Build strong partnerships with the PMO, Transformation Office, and Centers of Excellence to ensure that change management is fully integrated across the organization's strategic initiatives with the shared goal of building key organisational capabilities including change. These partnerships help the CMO position itself as a value-adding function rather than an operational overhead. This topic will be addressed in more depth in the following chapter. In essence the clearer the organisations vision and strategy is around organisational change capability, the more collective ownership there will be in driving it. A CMO that stands alone can be success at maintaining itself for a short duration but will fundamentally struggle if the goal is organisational change capability building focused on value.

Strategic use of Change Playbooks

A Change Playbook is a vital tool for organisational change that is predictable and repeated with small amounts of variation. This strategy and tool are great in the early days of a CMO, where there is very little change capability already in the organisation and where success stories need to be created. It fits directly into the defined CMO scope and is a great tool for creating change capability, democratising this with the teams involved in a particular repeated scenario like a merger in a company with an inorganic growth strategy. Change playbooks also opens up and almost passive cumulative return on investment as well as the one-time ROI coming from a first project.

Think on an IT implementation where we need to get a new tool adopted, or a re-organisation that always impacts governance, roles and responsibilities. Both scenarios offer slightly different playbook strategies. IT implementations are highly predictable in the timeline and requirements on the individual module implementation level, creating a playbook here can enable other roles to take over the work where possible freeing up an OCM consultant for more strategic work and creating more efficiency for the project by having less resources involved. A re-organisation on the other hand has a lot of complexity and requires strategic change management capability for success. A change playbook in this context will support all roles to understand a shared approach to managing the change, enable more roles to take responsibility and build change capability leaving a change manager to focus on more complex adoption and business needs. Both these scenarios support the democratisation of change capability to multiple roles in the organisation rather than keeping this for an elite few.

Besides being a vehicle for building organisational change maturity through democratising change capability, a playbook extends the return on investment from one-time to cumulative coming from re-use once established. A company with an inorganic growth strategy will do somewhere between 6- 10 mergers in a year.

The Change playbook serves as a critical tool for businesses seeking to build organizational change maturity and maximize return on investment (ROI) from their change initiatives. This structured guide enables organizations to standardize their change approach, reduce uncertainty, and optimize change execution while ensuring a cumulative impact over time. In this article, we will explore the role of a Change Playbook in enhancing organizational change maturity, its components, and the long-term benefits it delivers.

The traditional Change playbook very easily gets put on a virtual shelf somewhere collecting dust. But with the addition of value mapping and detailed scenarios it comes to life and becomes a hugely important tool in the kit of those aiming to increase ROI by managing change.

Future Outlook for CMOs and Upcoming Trends That Will Inform Strategy

While setting up a Change Management Office (CMO) is a significant achievement, maintaining its relevance in the long term requires ongoing innovation and adaptation. As organizational environments rapidly evolve, CMOs must stay agile by keeping pace with emerging trends and continuously refining their approach to driving value for the business. This involves not only staying current with broader external influences but also ensuring that the CMO evolves strategically to align with future demands.

Staying up to date with organizational and change-Shaping Trends is vital to remain effective, CMOs must actively track and respond to significant trends impacting both change management and organizational strategy. Among the most critical areas of focus are sustainability and ESG (Environmental, Social, and Governance) issues, which are increasingly shaping business priorities. As organizations strive to meet sustainability goals, CMOs must ensure that change initiatives align with broader corporate social responsibility (CSR) commitments. Whether driving environmental initiatives or fostering greater transparency in business practices, the CMO plays a pivotal role in ensuring that change management is aligned with sustainability objectives.

Additionally, artificial intelligence (AI) is transforming how businesses operate, and CMOs need to embrace AI-driven tools that can enhance the efficiency and accuracy of change management processes. Predictive analytics, for example, can forecast potential obstacles to change adoption, allowing CMOs to proactively address issues before they arise. AI can also automate certain aspects of change management, freeing up the CMO team to focus on more strategic tasks.

Alongside sustainability and AI, CMOs must remain aware of broader PESTLE factors—political, economic, social, technological, legal, and environmental influences—that can impact an organization's operating environment. By regularly assessing these factors, CMOs can better anticipate external challenges and tailor their change initiatives to navigate potential disruptions.

Innovating Next Steps Without Losing Sight of Value

While it is essential to stay informed about the future, it is equally critical for CMOs to avoid becoming overly speculative. Focusing on theoretical future trends can lead to a disconnect from the current realities of the organization. Therefore, CMOs should prioritize pragmatic innovation, driven by measurable value creation. This means regularly assessing whether new strategies, technologies, or methods contribute to tangible outcomes that benefit the organization, rather than simply implementing them because they are trending.

To ensure ongoing relevance, CMOs should continue to focus on value realization. Every change initiative must be aligned with the organization's strategic objectives, and the CMO should continuously evaluate how its efforts contribute to ROI and long-term value. By using data-driven approaches to track and measure performance, CMOs can provide evidence-based recommendations that guide future initiatives, ensuring that the office remains a crucial part of the organization's strategic framework.

The future of CMOs lies in their ability to stay responsive to emerging trends while maintaining a clear focus on value. Whether adapting to sustainability demands, leveraging AI for smarter change management, or responding to evolving PESTLE factors, CMOs must innovate pragmatically. By aligning their evolution with measurable outcomes, CMOs can ensure they remain indispensable to the organization's ongoing success.

Chapter Conclusion:

In this chapter we looked at how different strategies can be applied depending on the type of CMO goals and scope being put in place. Each deep dive captures elements of four strategic pillars and it's good to always include elements of each pillar to maintain CMO health.

This chapter emphasizes that a CMO's success depends on its ability to align with strategic goals, deliver tangible results, and embed change management practices into the organization's core operations. By focusing on democratizing change capability, adopting a ChangeOps approach, and continuously evaluating performance, CMOs can maintain their relevance and become indispensable strategic partners.

In the next chapter, the theme will be internal and external collaboration. There are natural synergies between different departments with overlaps in activities. These overlaps can be seen as invitations for basic collaboration, deeper level partnerships and even integrations to streamlining the overall management of change in organisations.

References

- LaMarsh, Daryl. *Change Capability Assessment Model (CCAM)*. LaMarsh Global, 2019.
- Kanikani, Isolde. *Change Management During Unprecedented Times*. IGI Global, 2022.
- CMMI Institute. "Capability Maturity Model Integration." www. cmmiinstitute.com.
- Collins, Jim. *Good to Great: Why Some Companies Make the Leap... and Others Don't*. HarperBusiness, 2001.
- Drucker, Peter F. *The Effective Executive: The Definitive Guide to Getting the Right Things Done*. HarperBusiness, 2006.
- Hamel, Gary, and C.K. Prahalad. *Competing for the Future*. Harvard Business Review Press, 1994.
- Lafley, A.G., and Roger L. Martin. *Playing to Win: How Strategy Really Works*. Harvard Business Review Press, 2013.
- Rumelt, Richard P. *Good Strategy, Bad Strategy: The Difference and Why It Matters*. Crown Business, 2011.

Chapter 8

Collaboration with Other Organizational Functions

A CMO can't be effective in its goal to build organisational change capability without collaboration. This chapter deep dives into different types of collaboration and partnership. Exploring general best practices as well as specific partnerships like those with the transformation office of PMO if present in the company.

Best Practices for Effective Collaboration

Based on the experiences of these organizations, several best practices can be identified for effective collaboration between the CMO and other functions:

1. **Engage Stakeholders Early and Often:** Involve stakeholders from the outset of change initiatives and maintain regular communication throughout the process. Early engagement helps secure support and ensures that all perspectives are considered. An engagement plan can be a useful tool here which can be as simple as an excel or 1-2 slides capturing all those that need to be engaged for CMO success. Adding information like their interests, frequency and type of contact including any personal information and preferences gathered over time.

2. **Develop Clear Goals, Roles and Responsibilities:** Clearly define the roles and responsibilities of each function involved in managing change initiatives. This clarity helps avoid confusion and ensures that all activities are coordinated. The previously mentioned RACI tool can be a great way to capture these roles and responsibilities, particularly if there is a high level of overlap on the day-to-day work. Charters for each partner can be another way to go, with any shared processes mapped out for easy reference by all.

3. **Foster a Culture of Collaboration around change capability development:** Promote a culture that values collaboration and open communication. Encourage team members to share ideas, provide feedback, and work together to achieve common goals. The CMO would often be the natural unit to lead strategic planning and execution of change capability exercises, in the same way the PMO does this for project change. Within change capability building there are multiple owners of particular types of change to work with and bring together into the mix.

4. **Utilize Shared Tools and Methodologies:** Adopt shared tools and methodologies to ensure consistency and facilitate collaboration. This approach helps streamline processes and enhances the effectiveness of change management practices. Integration of different capabilities is important for really making progress, but in a siloed state they are easier to understand and develop. Having the one way to talk about change is vital for growing a language that all can use no matter the context, and while siloing this change capability an seem like a good idea during inception, it is important to quickly integrate it in other capabilities so it becomes shared.

5. **Continuously Monitor and Improve:** Regularly monitor the effectiveness of collaboration efforts and make necessary adjustments. Gather feedback from stakeholders and use lessons learned to refine collaboration strategies and enhance overall performance.

Synergies between CMO and Other Functions based on management of change

Collaboration is essential for the success of the Change Management Office (CMO). To effectively manage and implement change initiatives, the CMO must work closely with other key organizational functions, such as the Project Management Office (PMO), Transformation Office, and Value Management Office.

Project Management Office (PMO):

The PMO is responsible for overseeing and coordinating project activities across the organization. It ensures that projects are completed on time, within budget, and meet quality standards. The PMO often has a strategic role, aligning projects with the organization's goals and providing a structured approach to project management.

Alignment with PMO:

- **Integrated Planning:** Collaborate on integrated planning to ensure that change management activities are incorporated into project plans. This alignment helps ensure that change initiatives are executed efficiently and effectively.
- **Resource Sharing:** Share resources, such as tools, templates, and expertise, to enhance the capabilities of both the CMO and PMO.
- **Joint Reporting:** Develop joint reporting mechanisms to track the progress and impact of change initiatives and projects. This approach provides a comprehensive view of organizational performance.

Transformation Office:

The Transformation Office is typically responsible for managing large-scale transformation initiatives that involve significant changes to the organization's structure, processes, or culture. These initiatives often span multiple departments and require coordinated efforts to achieve strategic objectives.

Alignment with Transformation Office:

- **Coordinated Strategies:** Work together to develop coordinated strategies for managing large-scale transformation initiatives. This collaboration ensures that change management efforts are aligned with the overall transformation goals.
- **Shared Leadership:** Establish shared leadership structures to oversee transformation initiatives, ensuring that both change management and transformation perspectives are considered in decision-making.
- **Combined Communication Plans:** Develop combined communication plans to ensure consistent messaging and stakeholder engagement throughout the transformation process.

Value Management Office:

The Value Management Office focuses on ensuring that change initiatives deliver measurable value to the organization. It involves evaluating the benefits and costs of change initiatives, tracking performance metrics, and ensuring that projects align with the organization's strategic goals and deliver expected outcomes.

Alignment with Value Management Office:

- **Value Tracking:** Collaborate on tracking the value delivered by change initiatives, ensuring that the benefits are measured and reported accurately.
- **Performance Metrics:** Develop shared performance metrics to evaluate the success of change initiatives and their impact on organizational goals.
- **Continuous Improvement:** Work together to identify opportunities for continuous improvement, leveraging insights from value management assessments to refine change management practices.

The CMO can leverage synergies with other organizational functions to enhance its effectiveness. By collaborating closely with the PMO, Transformation Office, and Value Management Office, the CMO can ensure that change initiatives are well-coordinated, aligned with strategic goals, and deliver measurable value.

Activities for Effective Collaboration

To facilitate effective collaboration between the CMO and other organizational functions, several frameworks and approaches can be utilized:

1. **Integrated Governance Structures:**
    - Steering Committees: Establish steering committees that include representatives from the CMO, PMO, Transformation Office, and Value Management Office. These committees provide oversight and ensure alignment across functions.

- Cross-Functional Teams: Create cross-functional teams to work on specific change initiatives, ensuring that all relevant perspectives are considered and that efforts are coordinated.

2. **Joint Planning and Coordination Meetings:**
   - Regular Coordination Meetings: Hold regular coordination meetings to discuss progress, address challenges, and ensure alignment across functions. These meetings help maintain open communication and foster collaboration.
   - Integrated Planning Sessions: Conduct integrated planning sessions to develop coordinated plans for change initiatives, projects, and transformation efforts. This approach ensures that all activities are aligned with strategic goals and resources are utilized effectively.

3. **Shared Tools and Methodologies:**
   - Standardized Tools: Develop standardized tools and templates that can be used by the CMO, PMO, Transformation Office, and Value Management Office. This approach ensures consistency and facilitates collaboration.
   - Common Methodologies: Adopt common methodologies for managing change initiatives, projects, and transformation efforts. This approach provides a unified framework for collaboration and enhances the effectiveness of change management practices.

4. **Combined Performance Metrics and Reporting:**
   - Shared KPIs: Define shared key performance indicators (KPIs) to measure the success of change initiatives, projects, and transformation efforts. This approach provides a comprehensive view of organizational performance.
   - Integrated Reporting: Develop integrated reporting mechanisms that combine data from the CMO, PMO, Transformation Office, and Value Management Office. This approach ensures that all relevant information is considered and provides a holistic view of progress and impact.

Case studies: Ways of creating Synergy

Several organizations have successfully leveraged collaboration between the CMO and other functions to drive effective change initiatives. These examples highlight the benefits of a coordinated approach and provide valuable insights into best practices.

Case Study 1: A lone standing CMO

In organisations where there aren't any other significant change managing units, the CMO has an open space to establish change capability. Collaborations are still vital but there's little negotiation around the strategy for change capability building itself. The scenario can also be the basis for developing a PMO or other capabilities within it, providing for a fully integrated change capability with the CMO encapsulating other units. Lastly before diving into an example, it is good to mention that this is the scenario where most of the contents of this book can be directly applied without too much tailoring.

A newly formed global business services (GBS) organization, delivering essential support functions to a multinational insurance group, faced the challenge of building change capability while also establishing its own foundational operations. The GBS comprised key functional areas including Finance, HR, IT, Legal, and Operations & Business Administration, catering to independent businesses within the group ranging from 10 to 1,000 employees each, spread across multiple regions globally.

Recognizing the critical role of change in ensuring long-term success, leadership approved the setup of a Change Management Office (CMO) with a broad scope focused on three pillars:

1. **Driving GBS Transformation**: Supporting the organization's growth towards achieving long-term strategic goals.

2. **Establishing Operational Excellence**: Ensuring the effective delivery of GBS services and managing foundational IT and HR transformation initiatives. To be extended into further operations infrastructure, once fully setup.

3. **Building Organizational Change Capability**: Strengthening resilience and adaptability across all business units to build

increased organisational resilience in the face of major change and agility to deal with unexpected market shifts.

Challenges & Strategic Approach: With the GBS itself being less than two years old, the CMO needed to navigate a complex environment where basic structures and governance were still being implemented. Early-stage IT and HR initiatives such as setting up an IT Service Management (ITSM) platform and HRIS ticketing system, were among the first major change projects that the CMO had to support under its third pillar of establishing operations. To drive success, the CMO adopted a strategic approach leveraging the following core methodologies:

- **Change Playbooks:** Implementing structured processes and scenario-based strategies for repeatable, scalable change execution. The scenarios of IT implementation project and Employee happiness (improvement project for Employee lifecycle management) were setup as targeted success areas.

- **ChangeOps and the Think Big, Act Pragmatic:** Aligning with long-term transformation goals while delivering quick wins that demonstrated immediate value. Each projects outcomes where embedded into continuous improvement and reporting with an appropriate cadence.

- **Democratizing Change:** Empowering employees across departments with role-specific change management skills. This took the form of onboarding employees to individual change capability building and roles specific change value realisation training later integrated into the newly structured employee lifecycle planning.

By using ChangeOps with its focus on value and overall change capability building as the connector between the three pillars, the CMO ensured seamless integration of transformation efforts, operational change, and long-term capability building.

Key Outcomes & Impact: The data-driven approach and maturity assessment framework used by the CMO helped showcase the tangible value of structured change management. The CMO successfully:

- **Delivered early operational success** by supporting IT and HR transformations, enabling smoother employee experiences across the insurance group.

- **Built foundational change capability** by embedding change skills across GBS functions, reducing resistance to new systems and processes.
- **Proved value through data-driven insights**, demonstrating how change management improved adoption rates, reduced project risks, and increased operational efficiency.

As a result of these successes, the CMO gained executive trust and was tasked with expanding its role by establishing both the Transformation Office (pillar 1) and PMO (pillar 3) within the GBS. This positioned the CMO as the central hub for governance, project execution, and strategic transformation efforts aligning on a single change capability strategy going forwards.

Conclusion

By taking a holistic, structured, and pragmatic approach, the CMO became a critical enabler of change maturity, operational efficiency, and long-term transformation within the GBS. Through the alignment of change capability building, structured transformation, and operational excellence, the CMO not only secured its place in the organization but expanded its influence to drive enterprise-wide strategic change.

Case Study 2: stablishing a Change Management Office in a Global Manufacturing Company

A global manufacturing company specializing in warehouse automation solutions, including package sorting and distribution, faced a major strategic transformation. With headquarters in the Netherlands and five global hubs, the company operated as a daughter company within a larger group.

Historically, the company followed a make-to-order (MTO) approach, designing fully customized warehouse solutions from scratch for each client. While this allowed for extreme customization, it was slow, expensive, and did not align with evolving customer demands. Over time, customers became less willing to pay for such customization, instead preferring faster, more standardized solutions. To remain competitive, the company decided to transition to a configure-to-order (CTO) approach, where standardized, modular components would be used to build warehouse solutions with greater efficiency and lower costs.

This transformation required a fundamental shift in how the company operated, affecting job architecture, governance, operating models, and cultural mindsets. Employees, particularly engineers, were concerned that moving to CTO would eliminate jobs, reduce creativity, and diminish the technical complexity of their work. These cultural concerns, combined with long-standing project-based operations and entrenched ways of working, created a high level of resistance.

To manage this transformation effectively, the company established a Change Management Office (CMO), also called the Change Team and Center of Excellence (CoE), to lead the change effort.

Setting Up the Change Management Office (CMO): The CMO was structured as a hybrid model, consisting of two senior change managers at HQ and newly appointed change managers in each of the five global hub locations. The primary objectives of the CMO were to:

1. Build organizational change capability through role-specific training.
2. Support and coordinate the transition from Make-to-Order (MTO) to Configure-to-Order (CTO).
3. Facilitate cultural shifts across the organization to align with the new way of working.

Several existing organizational functions were leveraged to enhance the CMO's impact:

- **Global Communications Team:** Strong internal communications capabilities ensured clear, transparent messaging about the transformation.
- **Learning & Development (L&D) Team**: A well-established Learning Council helped coordinate training programs across departments.
- **Project Management Office (PMO):** Although the PMO followed a heavy, outdated Prince2 methodology, it was well-respected and deeply embedded in operations. The CMO worked with the PMO to modernize project methodologies and integrate change management into project workflows.

While the PMO initially housed the CMO, it became clear that the PMO lacked strategic influence, which limited the effectiveness of change management initiatives. Over time, the CMO was integrated into the Global Communications and Learning & Development teams, with direct sponsorship from the CEO and CHRO.

Key Change Strategies Implemented:

To drive the MTO to CTO transformation and embed change capability across the organization, the CMO employed the following key strategies:

1. Change Capability Building: The CMO developed role-specific change training to equip employees at all levels with the necessary skills to navigate change. Training programs were tailored to:

- **Program and Project Managers**: Coached in change leadership and later tasked with training their peers.
- **Departmental Leads**: Given structured guidance on driving change within their teams.
- **Engineers & Operational Staff:** Provided with hands-on training on how CTO would work in practice, focusing on maintaining creativity within a structured framework.
- **Conclusion**: This approach democratized change management, ensuring that change capability was embedded throughout the organization rather than centralized within a small team.

2. Change Playbook for Cultural Shift: Recognizing the diverse cultural differences across the five global hubs, the CMO developed a change playbook customized for each location.

- In some locations, resistance was rooted in job security concerns, requiring focused efforts on retraining and reskilling employees.
- In others, the challenge was adapting from a highly autonomous working culture to a more standardized global framework.
- **Conclusion:** The localized playbooks provided structured guidance on navigating the transition while maintaining local strengths and fostering global alignment.

3. Integrating ChangeOps & Modernizing the PMO: Given the historically strong project culture, the PMO played a crucial role in executing change initiatives. However, its reliance on a rigid, outdated Prince2 methodology made it difficult to support iterative and continuous improvements needed for CTO adoption. To address this, the CMO introduced:

- A dedicated program stream to modernize the PMO, streamlining project methodologies to be more agile and adaptable.
- A Continuous Improvement (CI) framework that would gradually shift responsibility for iterative process enhancements away from project teams, allowing change to become an ongoing operational capability rather than something dependent solely on projects.
- ChangeOps integration, ensuring that change management efforts were embedded into project governance structures, creating a seamless connection between transformation initiatives and business-as-usual improvements.

4. Change Meter & Employee Ownership of Change: To reinforce broad-based engagement with change, the CMO introduced a Change Meter, an interactive tool that allowed employees to:

- Track their individual change progress.
- Provide real-time feedback on change initiatives.
- Access self-paced learning modules to build their own change capability.
- **Conclusion:** This increased employee ownership of change, helping shift the perception of CTO from a top-down mandate to a collaborative transformation effort.

Challenges & Lessons Learned: While the transition to Configure-to-Order (CTO) was ultimately successful, it was not without challenges:

1. **Early resistance from engineers:** Addressed through continuous upskilling and emphasizing the creative problem-solving aspects of CTO.
2. **Initial misalignment within the PMO:** Overcome by embedding ChangeOps, modernizing methodologies, and shifting

146

towards continuous improvement.

3. **Integration of the CMO within the organization**: Solved by transitioning sponsorship from the PMO to Global Communications & Learning & Development, with executive-level sponsorship from the CEO and CHRO.

Key Outcomes & Business Impact: After 18 months, the company successfully transitioned 70% of its product offerings to a Configure-to-Order model, significantly improving delivery speed, cost efficiency, and customer satisfaction. Additionally, the CMO's capability-building efforts resulted in:

- A 40% reduction in resistance to CTO adoption, measured through employee feedback surveys.
- An increase in project success rates, as ChangeOps integration reduced project rework and delays.
- A 30% increase in operational efficiency, as standardized processes freed up employees from excessive project-based customization work.

The CMO also successfully positioned itself as a long-term strategic enabler, leading to its expanded role in shaping future business transformation efforts.

Case study Conclusion: By aligning its approach with both business strategy and employee needs, the CMO successfully navigated cultural resistance, modernized project methodologies, and embedded change capability across the organization. The integration of ChangeOps, change playbooks, and role-based capability building ensured that change was not just an initiative but a core organizational competency. Ultimately, this structured, scalable approach positioned the company to remain competitive in an evolving market, delivering faster, more efficient solutions while maintaining the creativity and expertise that defined its engineering culture.

Chapter Conclusion:

In this chapter we looked at how a CMO can be integrated into an organisation setting it up for building change capability. Through integrations, partnerships and close collaborations the CMO drives change. How the CMO gets integrated is of vital importance and greatly influences everything from governance and modus operandi to sponsors and important scope. A standalone CMO described in case study 1 of this chapter is something of an ideal when it comes to implementing CMO best practices. Case study 2 showed that there was a shift of integration point from a less than strategic PMO to clear strategic sponsorship. In practice, many CMO find themselves integrated into other units which means that there is a strong dependency on how that unit is setup for success.

Effective collaboration between the Change Management Office (CMO) and other organizational functions is essential for the success of change initiatives. By understanding the roles and responsibilities of the PMO, Transformation Office, and Value Management Office, and leveraging synergies between these functions, the CMO can enhance its effectiveness and drive successful change efforts. Utilizing frameworks for collaboration, enhancing communication and coordination, and learning from real-world examples provide valuable insights into best practices. By fostering a culture of collaboration, developing clear roles and responsibilities, and continuously monitoring and improving collaboration efforts, organizations can ensure that their CMOs deliver sustained strategic success.

In the next chapter, the theme will be exploring the available toolkit for a CMO and how the multitude of frameworks, methods and models can support success realisation of CMO goals and scope.

References:

- Goldratt, Eliyahu M. *The Goal: A Process of Ongoing Improvement*. North River Press, 1984.

- Kaplan, Robert S., and David P. Norton. *The Balanced Scorecard: Translating Strategy into Action*. Harvard Business Review Press, 1996.

- Porter, Michael E. *Competitive Advantage: Creating and Sustaining Superior Performance*. Free Press, 1985.

- Rother, Mike. *Toyota Kata: Managing People for Improvement, Adaptiveness, and Superior Results*. McGraw-Hill, 2009.

- Deloitte. *The PMO Maturity Curve: How to Maximize Project Management Effectiveness*. Deloitte Insights, 2021.

- Gartner. *Evolving the Role of the Transformation Office to Drive Business Outcomes*. Gartner, 2022.

- PMI. *The Standard for Program Management*. Project Management Institute, 2017.

Chapter 9

CMO Toolkit: Models, Theories, and Approaches Influencing CMOs

Change Management Offices (CMOs) can utilize a variety of models, theories, and approaches to guide their activities and ensure effective change management in the broadest most holistic sense. These frameworks provide structured methodologies, best practices, and theoretical underpinnings that help CMOs navigate the complexities of organizational change.

This chapter is designed in such a way as to be a mini change bible of possible best practices that can be used, and is certainly not suggesting that all should be put into a change practice. At the same time as referencing these trustworthy sources for change best practice, it's also important to keep in mind that some are fairly dated and not necessarily fitting organisations needs in these fast-paced times. Those considered to directly lend themselves to a modern CMO are shared in the first section, followed by a more extensive list shared in dictionary form with reference to their potential use in change capability building.

Frameworks, standards and Toolkit for the modern CMO

Cynefin Framework: Navigating Complexity in Change Management

The Cynefin Framework, developed by Dave Snowden, is a decision-making and sense-making model that categorizes problems into five domains: Clear, Complicated, Complex, Chaotic, and Disorder. The framework draws on systems theory and helps organizations navigate uncertainty and complexity by identifying the appropriate approach to different types of challenges guiding the decision-making approach.

The fact that the framework incorporates all types of change into one framework, makes this an extremely elegant basis for developing further change strategies, methods and approaches which is why it is being presented here in this section. Most linear change management methods fit easily into the simple and complicated change types. Disorder accounts for the fact that sometimes the nature of the change is unknown and the further areas of complex and chaotic require very different approach to how one thinks about change. For those who challenge whether change is ever truly managed are probably referring to these last two areas.

Key Areas Related to Change Management

1. Clear (Simple) Change: Well-defined processes where best practices and standard operating procedures (SOPs) are sufficient. Example: Implementing a routine software update.
2. Complicated Change: Requires expert analysis and multiple possible solutions but remains predictable. Example: Large-scale ERP implementation.
3. Complex Change: The outcome is unpredictable, requiring an adaptive, iterative approach. Example: Cultural transformation across a global organization.
4. Chaotic Change: Requires immediate action and strong leadership to stabilize the situation. Example: Crisis management or sudden regulatory shifts.
5. Disorder: When it is unclear which domain a problem fits into, requiring further analysis.

Why the Cynefin Framework is Essential for a CMO

- Many traditional change management models (e.g., ADKAR, Kotter's 8 Steps) work best in Clear and Complicated domains but struggle in Complex or Chaotic environments.
- Cynefin helps CMOs adapt their strategy based on the type of change, ensuring that they don't apply rigid methodologies where agility and emergent solutions are needed.
- It connects seamlessly with systems thinking, emphasizing holistic change management instead of treating change as a linear process.

- The Cynefin framework is a very light way to holistically manage change, recognising the need for different approaches and ways of working with change.

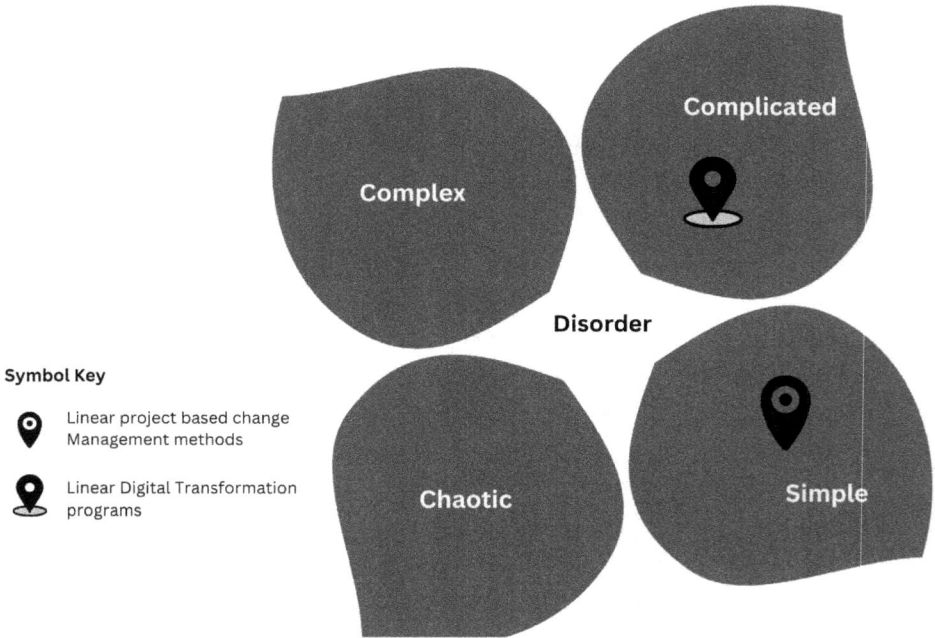

Complicated

Complex

Disorder

Symbol Key

⦿ Linear project based change Management methods

⚲ Linear Digital Transformation programs

Chaotic

Simple

Figure 13: showing Cynefin change decision framework and where the linear methods and programs fit on this. Cynefin framework provides a much more holistic view of the different types of change we can come across, and through this an interesting framework to base change strategy on. There is a tendency to manage change the same way with the same methods and then when it gets a little complex start creating new and innovative approaches. Working with a universal framework like Cynefin would allow us to establish approaches to change capability building and management that cover all areas. Creating a flexible tool kit fit for purpose, rather than misusing methods that can never successfully achieve success in areas they are not designed for.

Artificial Intelligence (AI) in Change Management

AI is not one single technology but an umbrella term covering multiple innovation areas that are currently moving very fast. Gartner promotes the idea that there are two development tracks. The first which includes technology developers, is fast and furious driven by a need to be first to market new AI capabilities. The second group however includes the end-user group which including organisations, moves at a lot slower paced and is based on the adoption of the new technology. This is very useful way to separate end-users from the need for speed and start to tackle the particular use cases where AI can support.

For CMOs, understanding AI's practical applications is critical for supporting business transformation and improving change processes. The CMO team is both a direct end-user and a facilitator of end-users if working on AI driven transformation initiatives. As end-users, the CMO can probably most directly use GenAI to support content creation and save time on manual tasks. Organisational network analysis also provides an already tried and tested approach to working with networked views of the organisation, and chatbots have been wides used to support adoption of new knowledge and provide personalised change coaching. These are all tools at the disposal of the CMO.

From the perspective of the CMO facilitating AI transformations, it's important to develop a more than basic understanding of the capacity of AI types enough to tangify this for users so they can engage and adopt. Currently there appears to be a huge drive for organisations to adopt AI, and at the same time barriers of trust and a lack of clarity on how this can realise value get in the way of real progress. The suggestion for any CMO facilitating AI changes, is to break down the actual organisational need or goal for value being addressed, then search for the right tools to achieve it. AI might or might not be in this tool kit.

Key Areas of AI That Impact Change Management (not exhaustive):

1. **Generative AI (GenAI)**: AI models that create text, images, or code. Example: AI-generated communication plans for change initiatives.
2. **Agentic AI**: AI agents that operate autonomously based on pre-defined goals. Example: AI-driven automation of organizational change assessments.

3. **AI-Driven Knowledge Graphs:** AI-powered repositories that structure company knowledge, enhance the development of different organisational capabilities and acts like a map to further building career paths and job architecture, service blue prints and other value flows. The same construct can also be used to understand organisational risk, and interdependencies between departments.

4. **Organisational Network Analysis (ONA):** Uses AI and graph theory to map relationships and identify key influencers for change initiatives. While this is a basic use when working with the people and relations view, the same setup can be used to map collaborations between departments, assess organisational silos and bottle necks. Goldratt's theory of constraints gives a great approach to managing outcomes once analysed.

5. **AI for Organisational Change Capability Building:** AI-driven adaptive learning systems can tailor change training for individuals based on role and skill gaps. While these tools have more or less been around for a longer time, the fact that they are now readily available for use makes a huge difference in making the goal of building organisational change capability an attainable one and not simply theoretical which was the perception by many in conversations on the topic 10+ years ago. We can now use data and AI to tangify almost anything within an organisation provided that the data quality and compliance issues (e.g. GDPR) don't get in the way.

Why AI is Essential for a CMO

- AI enhances decision-making by analysing vast amounts of change data.
- Helps predict resistance patterns and tailor interventions based on employee sentiment.
- AI-powered change analytics dashboards allow real-time tracking of transformation progress.
- AI enables personalized change management strategies, improving employee engagement.

Customer-Centric Models in Change Management

A customer-centric approach ensures that change initiatives prioritize the needs of both external and internal customers, including employees, business partners, and external contractors. For a CMO to be effective, it must map and manage change in a way that enhances customer experiences, reduces friction, and fosters engagement across all stakeholder groups.

Key Areas Related to Customer-Centric Change Management

1. **Customer Journey Mapping**: A method for visualizing how customers experience services and interactions across different touchpoints. This enables CMOs to:
   - Identify pain points in change initiatives.
   - Enhance the transition experience during strategic transformations.
   - Ensure seamless stakeholder engagement at critical touchpoints.

2. **Voice of the Customer (VoC)**: A structured approach to gathering and analysing customer feedback, which helps CMOs:
   - Understand stakeholder concerns and expectations.
   - Make data-driven decisions about managing change impact.
   - Adjust strategies to maintain stakeholder satisfaction.

3. **Customer Experience Management (CEM)**: Focuses on optimizing customer interactions to:
   - Ensure loyalty and satisfaction during change efforts.
   - Enhance engagement across different customer segments.
   - Foster long-term relationships with employees and external partners.

4. **Design Thinking Approaches**: A problem-solving method that involves collaborative, iterative prototyping to:
   - Test and refine new ways of managing change.

- Develop flexible, user-centred solutions for non-linear change initiatives.
- Empower teams to experiment with process improvements before full implementation.

Why a Customer-Centric Approach Is Essential for CMOs

- **Ensures Adoption**: Change initiatives that align with customer needs are more likely to be embraced and sustained.
- **Reduces Resistance**: Addressing customer pain points lowers friction and improves stakeholder engagement.
- **Enhances Change Impact**: A customer-first perspective aligns transformation efforts with business success metrics.
- **Supports Agile Adaptation**: Non-linear change efforts require iterative approaches that continuously adjust based on real customer feedback.

By embedding customer-centric methodologies into the CMO strategy, organizations can drive more meaningful, well-adopted, and impactful change.

Lean Thinking & Goldratt's Theory of Constraints in Change Management

Lean Thinking, originating from Toyota's Production System (TPS), focuses on eliminating waste and maximizing value in organizational processes. Goldratt's Theory of Constraints (TOC) complements Lean by emphasizing identifying and addressing bottlenecks that limit performance.

Key Areas Related to Change Management

1. **Lean Change Management:** Streamlining change processes by removing inefficiencies.
2. **Identifying Constraints in Change Initiatives:** Using TOC to pinpoint bottlenecks in adoption and transformation efforts.
3. **Flow-Based Change Adoption:** Ensuring continuous flow of change activities rather than waiting for staged milestones.

Why Lean & TOC are Essential for a CMO

- Many CMOs struggle with bureaucratic, document-heavy approaches—Lean ensures pragmatic, high-impact execution.
- Helps CMOs prioritize change efforts by focusing on the biggest constraints limiting progress.
- Drives faster adoption and higher ROI by ensuring that change initiatives don't become overly complex and inefficient.

Value-Driven Approaches in Change Management

For a CMO to remain strategically relevant, it must focus on delivering measurable value rather than merely overseeing change processes. Value-driven approaches help CMOs prioritize efforts, ensuring that change initiatives align with organizational goals, stakeholder needs, and high-impact areas.

Key Areas Related to Value-Driven Change Management

1. **Value Proposition Canvas**: A framework that helps organizations define and articulate the value they deliver to customers, employees, and stakeholders.
2. **Value Mapping**: A structured approach to identifying:
   - Unmanaged change in critical business areas.
   - Change initiatives that generate waste due to redundancy, inefficiency, or poor execution.
   - Strategic priorities where structured change management is essential for success.
3. **Balanced Scorecard**: A tool for aligning change management efforts with overall business strategy, focusing on financial, customer, operational, and employee growth metrics.

Why Value-Driven Change Management Is Essential for a CMO

- **Prioritizes High-Impact Change:** Ensures that resources and attention are focused on the most valuable areas of transformation.
- **Avoids Change Waste:** Identifies change efforts that consume

157

effort but produce little business value, enabling better allocation of resources.

- **Enhances Executive Buy-In:** Demonstrates clear ROI and strategic alignment, making it easier to gain support and sponsorship.
- **Strengthens Decision-Making:** Provides a quantifiable framework for assessing which change initiatives deliver the greatest impact.

By embedding value-driven methodologies into the CMO strategy, organizations can ensure that change management is not just a function, but a value-generating discipline.

Change Management Tools for Streamlining Standardization and Driving a Data-Driven Approach

Managing change at scale requires more than just methodologies, it demands a toolkit that enables standardization, automation of repetitive tasks, and real-time data-driven insights. Without the right digital enablers, CMOs risk spending too much time on documentation rather than focusing on execution, adoption, and value realization. Change management applications can save a lot of time for a practitioner while enhancing the output of data for decision making. For a CMO growing a change practice, these tools can also support the growth of a shared approach driving change in organisations.

Key Areas Related to Change Management Tooling

1. **Standardized Change Toolkits:** Digital platforms that store, update, and automate the use of change templates (e.g., stakeholder assessments, impact analyses, change roadmaps).
2. **Change Portfolio Dashboards:** Tools that track change initiatives across the organization, visualizing risks, progress, and impact. These are a vital asset when it comes to showing value realisation and accomplishment of success criteria.
3. **Data-Driven Change Management:** AI-powered insights on employee sentiment, adoption trends, and intervention effectiveness.

4. **Automated Communications and Engagement Tracking:** Platforms that personalize communication based on resistance levels and stakeholder influence.

5. **Scenario-Based Playbooks:** Digital repositories that allow organizations to replicate successful change strategies, reducing rework in similar future initiatives.

Why Change Management Tools Are Essential for a CMO

- **Drives Consistency:** Ensures that change is managed in a repeatable and measurable way rather than relying on individual preferences.

- **Enhances Decision-Making:** Provides real-time insights into change adoption, allowing for quick course corrections.

- **Supports Agile Change Management:** Enables a dynamic approach to change, adapting strategies based on live data rather than assumptions. Enabling increased value realisation during projects and not just reporting on it at the end.

- **Enables Scaling:** Organizations with multiple change projects running in parallel can maintain oversight without excessive governance.

By integrating digital tools into the CMO strategy, organizations can shift from reactive change management to proactive, insight-driven transformation.

Extended Toolkit: Theories, Models, Frameworks, and Approaches for Organisational Change Capability Building

The below list is by no means exhaustive, but has been added to this chapter to openly share many of the influencing models and methods talked about in the second chapter and which are fused into more practitioners approaches to change. See the below list as one for inspiration, or a checklist for when the CMO is building its own body of knowledge and capability.

Leadership Theories

- **Transformational Leadership Theory** – Focuses on leaders who inspire, motivate, and drive innovation and change. Helps CMOs create a vision-driven change culture.
- **Servant Leadership** – Leaders prioritize the needs of their team to foster collaboration and growth. Encourages inclusive leadership in CMOs.
- **Situational Leadership** – Leaders adjust their style based on the maturity and readiness of their team. Supports flexible leadership for diverse change initiatives.
- **Transactional Leadership** – Focuses on structured policies, rewards, and punishments to drive behaviour. Provides a compliance-driven approach for CMOs in regulated industries.
- **Adaptive Leadership** – Leaders encourage adaptation and learning in complex, uncertain environments. Helps CMOs navigate evolving business landscapes.
- **Charismatic Leadership** – Relies on personal charm and vision to lead change. Effective for CMOs to rally support for transformation.
- **Authentic Leadership** – Leader's act with self-awareness, integrity, and transparency. Builds trust in change initiatives.
- **Ethical Leadership** – Focuses on making morally sound decisions in leadership. Essential for governance and sustainability-driven change.
- **Distributed Leadership** – Leadership responsibilities are shared across teams. Encourages decentralized change adoption.
- **Level 5 Leadership (Jim Collins)** – Leader's blend humility with professional will to drive success. Helps CMOs build enduring organizational change capability.

Change Management frameworks and Models

- **ACMP's The Global standard for change management:** This is a method agnostic standard for change management that includes a code of ethics for practitioners and forms the basis of the CCMP professional certification.

- **Kotter's 8-Step Change Model** – Provides a roadmap for successful transformation. Aligns CMO efforts with structured phases of change.
- **Lewin's Change Management Model** – Breaks change into Unfreeze, Change, and Refreeze. Helps CMOs manage resistance effectively.
- **Bridges' Transition Model** – Focuses on psychological transitions of individuals in change. Aids CMOs in addressing employee adaptation.
- **Prosci's ADKAR Model** – Focuses on individual change through Awareness, Desire, Knowledge, Ability, and Reinforcement. Supports structured capability-building initiatives.
- **The Change Curve (Kubler-Ross)** – Models emotional responses to change. Supports CMOs in change impact assessment.
- **McKinsey 7-S Framework** – Ensures alignment of strategy, structure, and culture. Helps CMOs embed change across key organizational elements.
- **Accelerating Implementation Methodology (AIM)** – Focuses on execution and adoption of change. Provides CMOs with an implementation roadmap.
- **The Deming Cycle (PDCA)** – Plan-Do-Check-Act ensures continuous improvement. Integrates well with iterative change approaches.
- **Six Batteries of Change** – Measures organizational energy for change. Helps CMOs assess change readiness.
- **Rogers' Diffusion of Innovations Model** – Explains how new ideas spread. Guides CMOs in structuring adoption strategies.

Organizational Development & Capability Models

- **C+MMF (Change & Maturity Management Framework)** – Maps key capabilities and change maturity levels. Helps CMOs prioritize capability-building efforts.
- **Capability Maturity Model (CMMI)** – Defines capability levels for process maturity. Supports CMOs in structured improvement initiatives.

- **The Learning Organization (Peter Senge)** – Encourages continuous learning as a competitive advantage. Aids CMOs in fostering adaptability.
- **Organizational Network Analysis (ONA)** – Uses graph theory to map informal networks. Helps CMOs leverage key influencers in change.
- **Graph Theory & Network Science** – Analyses relationships between organizational nodes. Supports CMOs in managing stakeholder dynamics.
- **Cynefin Framework** – Helps classify problems into simple, complicated, complex, or chaotic. Guides CMOs in choosing appropriate change strategies.
- **Appreciative Inquiry (AI)** – Focuses on strengths-based change. Encourages CMOs to build on existing organizational capabilities.
- **Nudge Theory** – Uses behavioural economics to subtly encourage change. Helps CMOs influence change adoption with minimal resistance.
- **Gossip Theory** – Examines the informal communication networks within organizations. Helps CMOs address cultural resistance.
- **Social Cognitive Theory (Bandura)** – Highlights observational learning and role modelling. Supports CMOs in leadership-driven change.

Operational & Process Improvement Frameworks

- **Lean Management** – Focuses on eliminating waste and improving efficiency. Ensures CMOs integrate change with operational excellence.
- **Six Sigma** – Uses data-driven methods to improve process quality. Supports CMOs in reducing errors during transformation.
- **Total Quality Management (TQM)** – Encourages continuous organizational improvement. Helps CMOs foster a culture of excellence.
- **Business Process Reengineering (BPR)** – Redesigns workflows

for efficiency. Assists CMOs in large-scale operational changes.

- **Balanced Scorecard (Kaplan & Norton)** – Aligns business performance with strategic objectives. Helps CMOs track change effectiveness.
- **ISO 9001 Quality Management** – Establishes global quality management standards. Ensures CMOs maintain compliance during change.
- **Service Design Thinking** – Focuses on user experience in change implementation. Helps CMOs optimize change from an employee perspective.
- **Agile Change Management** – Uses iterative cycles for faster adaptation. Helps CMOs manage change in agile organizations.
- **DevOps & ChangeOps** – Integrates IT and operations for seamless deployment. Supports CMOs in technology-driven change.
- **Scenario Planning (Shell Method)** – Develops future-oriented strategies. Helps CMOs anticipate long-term change impacts.
- **The Toyota Production System (TPS)** – Introduces lean and just-in-time production principles. Helps CMOs drive operational efficiencies.
- **Theory of Constraints (Goldratt)** – Identifies bottlenecks in processes. Helps CMOs streamline change adoption across departments.

Group Dynamics, Learning & development, and Behavioural Science Approaches

- **Tuckman's Stages of Group Development** – Defines Forming, Storming, Norming, Performing. Helps CMOs facilitate team adaptation.
- **Hofstede's Cultural Dimensions** – Analyses national and organizational cultures. Helps CMOs tailor change strategies globally.
- **Organizational Culture Model (Schein)** – Identifies deep-seated cultural assumptions. Helps CMOs shape culture-driven transformation.

- **Job Demands-Resources Model** – Balances workload and support mechanisms. Helps CMOs improve change-related employee well-being.
- **Fiedler's Contingency Model** – Matches leadership style to situation. Supports CMOs in aligning leadership with change initiatives.
- **Cognitive Load Theory** – Explains how people process information. Helps CMOs design digestible change communications.
- **The SCARF Model (David Rock)** – Addresses brain-based responses to change. Helps CMOs reduce resistance.
- **Goal-Setting Theory (Locke & Latham)** – Links motivation to performance. Helps CMOs align change goals with business objectives.
- **Spiral Dynamics** – Maps cultural and value system shifts in organizations. Helps CMOs drive deep, systemic change.
- **Theory of Planned Behaviour (Ajzen)** – Examines how intention drives behaviour. Helps CMOs craft persuasive change strategies.
- **Blue Ocean Strategy** – Encourages market differentiation and strategic growth. Helps CMOs guide change towards competitive advantages.
- **Design Thinking** – Focuses on human-centric problem-solving. Supports CMOs in engaging stakeholders effectively.
- **The Viable System Model (VSM)** – A framework for organizational self-regulation and adaptability. Supports CMOs in resilience-building efforts.
- **Theory U (Otto Scharmer)** – Focuses on transformational leadership through deep listening and reflection. Helps CMOs drive sustainable change.
- **The Spiral of Experience (Kolb)** – Highlights experiential learning in professional growth. Supports CMOs in leadership development initiatives.

Motivation, Influencing, and Communication

- **Self-Determination Theory (Deci & Ryan)** – Explains how intrinsic and extrinsic motivation impact performance. Helps CMOs design engagement strategies for change.

- **Maslow's Hierarchy of Needs** – Highlights human motivation from basic needs to self-actualization. Helps CMOs align change messaging with employee concerns.

- **Expectancy Theory (Vroom)** – Suggests people act based on expected outcomes. Helps CMOs create incentive structures to drive adoption.

- **Influence Strategies (Cialdini)** – Covers principles of persuasion such as reciprocity, scarcity, and authority. Helps CMOs craft compelling communication plans.

- **Stakeholder Salience Model** – Prioritizes stakeholders based on power, urgency, and legitimacy. Helps CMOs manage engagement effectively.

- **Elaboration Likelihood Model** – Explains how individuals process persuasive messages. Helps CMOs tailor communication strategies.

- **Framing Theory** – Highlights how presenting information in different ways influences perception. Helps CMOs craft impactful change narratives.

- **Cognitive Dissonance Theory (Festinger)** – Explains how conflicting beliefs cause discomfort and behavioural shifts. Helps CMOs address resistance to change.

- **Communication Accommodation Theory** – Discusses how people adapt communication styles based on context. Helps CMOs improve stakeholder interactions.

- **Sensemaking Theory (Weick)** – Explains how individuals construct meaning from change experiences. Helps CMOs guide employees through uncertainty.

Chapter Conclusion:

In this chapter we looked at both a proposed kit for modern CMOs and an extended inspiration list. There are multiple tools out there in the form of established approaches, methods and toolkits. It's important to be discerning about which tools are fit for the purposes you need within the process of setting up the CMO. If for example, you have a broad scope CMO with heavy focus on building organisational maturity a model like McKinsey's 7s might be more appropriate than Prosci's ADKAR. Already established tools might not be able to keep up with the extreme increases of change, the need for efficient and effective management that we see today calling for losing these tools for something fit for these times. Tools are always a means to an end not the end itself and should be used sparingly.

As a big believer in using the tried and tested approaches already out there, there is also a growing need to develop a toolkit that is specific to change capability building on the organisational scale. Tools that were appropriate 20 or more years ago were built for that time and don't necessarily make sense now with the challenges we face today.

The next and last chapter will be bringing all the themes of this book together and sow seeds for further works on the topic of building organisational change capability. Setting up strategic CMOs is just one area within a much bigger body of research.

References:

- Christensen, Clayton M., and Michael E. Raynor. *The Innovator's Solution: Creating and Sustaining Successful Growth*. Harvard Business Review Press, 2003.

- Denning, Steve. *The Age of Agile: How Smart Companies Are Transforming the Way Work Gets Done*. HarperBusiness, 2018.

- Kim, W. Chan, and Renée Mauborgne. *Blue Ocean Strategy: How to Create Uncontested Market Space and Make the Competition Irrelevant*. Harvard Business Review Press, 2015.

- Ries, Eric. *The Lean Startup: How Today's Entrepreneurs Use Continuous Innovation to Create Radically Successful Businesses*. Crown Business, 2011.

- Rock, David. *Your Brain at Work: Strategies for Overcoming Distraction, Regaining Focus, and Working Smarter All Day Long*. HarperBusiness, 2009.

-

- Sinek, Simon. *Start With Why: How Great Leaders Inspire Everyone to Take Action*. Penguin, 2009.

- Thaler, Richard H., and Cass R. Sunstein. *Nudge: Improving Decisions About Health, Wealth, and Happiness*. Yale University Press, 2008.

- Waterman, Robert H., et al. *In Search of Excellence: Lessons from America's Best-Run Companies*. Harper & Row, 1982.

- Meyer, Erin. *The Culture Map: Breaking Through the Invisible Boundaries of Global Business*. PublicAffairs, 2014.

- Curtis, Bill, et al. *The People Capability Maturity Model: Guidelines for Improving the Workforce*. Addison-Wesley, 2009.

- Goldratt, Eliyahu M. *The Goal: A Process of Ongoing Improvement*. North River Press, 1984.

- Pink, Daniel H. *Drive: The Surprising Truth About What Motivates Us*. Riverhead Books, 2009.

- Newman, Henry. *The Changemaker Playbook: The New Physics of Leadership in a World of Disruption*. Harvard Business Review Press, 2021.

- Tuckman, Bruce W. "Developmental Sequence in Small Groups." *Psychological Bulletin*, vol. 63, no. 6, 1965, pp. 384-399.

- De Prins, Jef, and Peter De Prins. *Six Batteries of Change: Plug into the Energy of Your Organization*. LannooCampus, 2017.

- Cross, Rob, et al. *The Hidden Power of Social Networks: Understanding How Work Really Gets Done in Organizations*. Harvard Business Review Press, 2004.

Chapter 10

Concluding this book

This book has provided a comprehensive and strategic guide to establishing a Change Management Office (CMO) capable of driving meaningful and sustainable transformation in today's complex organizational landscapes. By weaving together foundational theories, contemporary models, and practical yet strategic approaches, this text serves as both a blueprint and a call to action for leaders aiming to embed change as a core organizational competency.

The journey began with an exploration of the history and evolution of CMOs, contextualizing their role within the broader organizational ecosystem. Originally emerging as tactical units to support individual change initiatives and change management maturity building, CMOs have a huge mostly untapped potential to evolve into strategic partners responsible for building organizational change maturity with the end goal of further supporting the organisation realise strategic value.

Future Outlook for CMOs

The role of the Change Management Office (CMO) is set to grow in complexity and strategic importance as organizations navigate an era of unprecedented change. Future-proof CMOs must evolve to meet emerging challenges and capitalize on new opportunities. By leveraging advanced technologies, addressing global priorities, and adopting an innovation-driven mindset, CMOs can ensure they remain relevant and impactful.

One of the most critical advancements for CMOs lies in the integration of AI-driven change analytics. Artificial intelligence offers tools to analyse data at scale, providing insights into organizational readiness, employee sentiment, and the effectiveness of change initiatives. These capabilities enable CMOs to make data-driven decisions, predict potential challenges, and personalize change strategies for diverse employee groups. AI's potential to streamline processes and enhance precision ensures that CMOs can remain agile and proactive in responding to organizational needs.

Another pivotal focus for CMOs is Environmental, Social, and Governance (ESG) initiatives, which are becoming integral to corporate strategy. As organizations align themselves with sustainable practices and socially responsible goals, CMOs must lead the charge in embedding ESG principles into the organizational fabric. By managing the changes necessary to adopt these priorities—such as restructuring operations for sustainability or enhancing diversity and inclusion initiatives—CMOs can ensure that ESG goals translate into actionable and measurable outcomes.

Innovation will remain a cornerstone of future CMOs, with this referring to pragmatic development of next steps filling gaps in our current change best practices and not getting lost in future theoretical possibilities. As hubs of transformation, CMOs must constantly refine their methodologies to address evolving challenges. This involves staying ahead of industry trends, experimenting with novel approaches, and fostering a culture of continuous improvement. The capacity to innovate ensures that CMOs can pivot strategies and tools to align with emerging technologies, shifts in market dynamics, and the expectations of an increasingly change-savvy workforce.

Flexibility will be essential for ensuring that CMO strategies, tools, and collaborations remain aligned with shifting organizational needs. Rigid methodologies risk falling short in dynamic environments; instead, CMOs must adopt frameworks that emphasize adaptability and iterative progress. This agility not only supports immediate change initiatives but also positions the CMO as a trusted advisor capable of steering organizations through long-term transformation.

The demand for effective change capabilities is set to grow as organizations face increasing levels of complexity and disruption. By continually evolving, CMOs can play a pivotal role in enhancing organizational agility, enabling teams to embrace change as a competitive advantage. The future promises an expanded role for CMOs, not merely as facilitators of change, but as strategic partners driving the organization's success in an unpredictable world.

In conclusion, the future of the CMO is one of boundless potential. Through innovation, adaptability, and a steadfast commitment to organizational growth, CMOs will not only navigate the complexities of change but shape the very strategies that define success in the years to come.

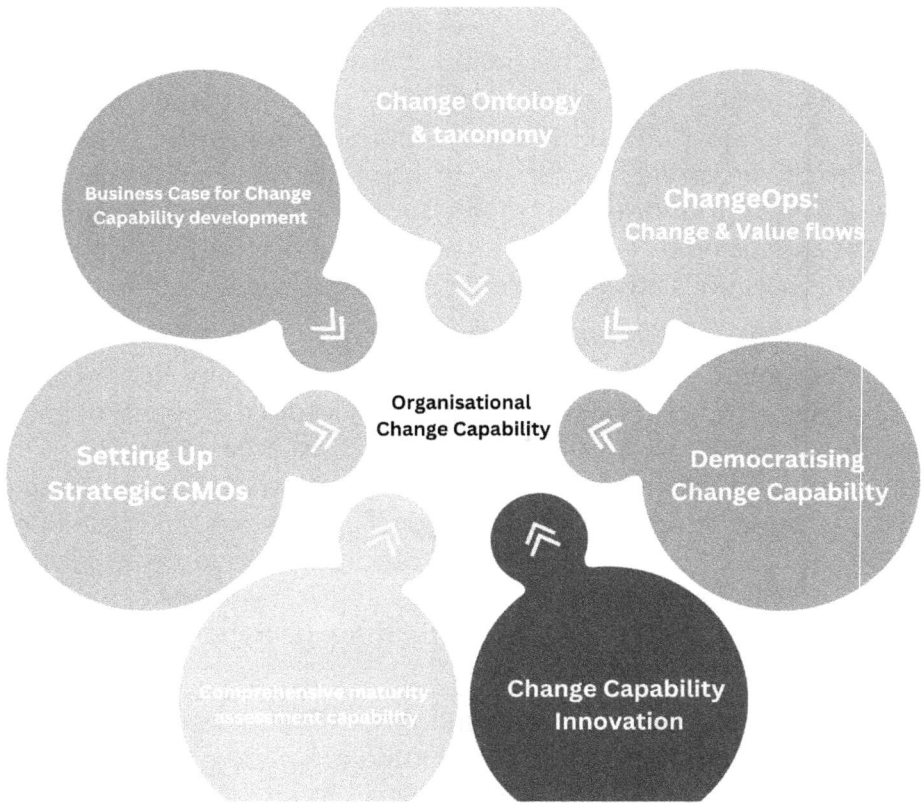

Figure 14: Showing the CMO as part of a bigger picture of organisational change maturity building tools and approaches.

Final Thoughts...

Strategic change management is essential for the long-term success of any organization. By establishing a well-structured CMO, organizations can better manage change, align with strategic goals, and achieve lasting benefits through the facilitation of change converting to an integrated value output. This is based on all capabilities intrinsically working together across the organisation, for the greater good of all individuals and the organisation.

The three headline takeaways for someone aiming to setup a strategic CMO, would be to focus on organisational change capability building fuelled by democratisation of change, strategic integration into the organisational structure and partner landscape. Last but not least, the vital role ChangeOps has in creating flow of change and value realisation through organisations. Shifting our mindset from one of a CMO being there to cater for a select few specialists to one where it is a thriving strategic partner to the business. Besides this, the recognition that a CMO or change capability centre of excellence is one very important part of a much larger and growing toolkit for building organisational change capability.

Appendices

Glossary of Key Terms

- **Center of Excellence (CoE):** A dedicated team or function that develops, standardizes, and promotes best practices, methodologies, and innovations in a specific discipline, ensuring continuous improvement across an organization.
- **Change Management:** The process of preparing, supporting, and helping individuals, teams, and organizations in making organizational change.
- **Change Management Office (CMO):** A centralized function responsible for overseeing and managing change initiatives within an organization.
- **Change Maturity Model:** A framework that assesses an organization's ability to manage change, outlining stages of maturity from ad-hoc and reactive to structured, embedded, and continuously improving change management practices.
- **ChangeOps:** The strategic harnessing of all types of change in the organization, operationalizing this into organizational value flows.
- **Chief Change Officer (CCO):** The leader of the CMO, responsible for driving change initiatives and overseeing the CMO team.
- **Community of Practice (CoP):** A group of professionals who share a common interest and collaborate to exchange knowledge, develop skills, and improve best practices in a specific domain.
- **Democratizing Change:** The strategy of building basic individual and role-specific change capability that empowers individuals throughout the organization to drive organizational change.
- **Digital Transformation:** The integration of advanced digital technologies into business processes, operations, and customer interactions to enhance efficiency, agility, and competitiveness.

- **Governance Framework:** A set of policies, structures, and decision-making processes that ensure change initiatives align with organizational objectives, regulatory requirements, and risk management standards.

- **Operating Model:** The blueprint that defines how an organization delivers value by structuring its processes, people, technology, and governance to execute strategy effectively and efficiently.

- **Organizational Change Capability:** The ability of an organization to continuously and effectively manage, implement, and sustain change initiatives through structured processes, leadership alignment, and employee engagement.

- **Organizational Design:** The structure, roles, workflows, and decision-making hierarchies within an organization that determine how work is coordinated and aligned with strategic goals.

- **Organizational Network Analysis (ONA):** A methodology used to map informal networks and relationships within an organization, identifying key influencers and bottlenecks in change adoption.

- **Organizational Resilience:** The ability of an organization to anticipate, respond to, and recover from disruptions while maintaining operational stability and competitive advantage.

- **Project Management Office (PMO):** A centralized function responsible for overseeing and managing projects within an organization.

- **Scenario-Based Change Playbook:** A structured framework that provides tailored strategies for recurring high-impact change scenarios, improving consistency, efficiency, and cumulative ROI from change initiatives.

- **Stakeholder Management:** The strategic process of identifying, analysing, engaging, and communicating with individuals or groups affected by or influencing a project, initiative, or change effort to ensure alignment and support.

- **Strategy:** A high-level plan that defines an organization's long-term goals, competitive positioning, and resource allocation to achieve sustainable success and business objectives.

- **Transformation Office (TO):** A function responsible for coordinating and managing large-scale transformation initiatives within an organization.
- **Value Management Office (VMO):** A function responsible for ensuring that change initiatives deliver measurable value to the organization.

Sample Templates, Frameworks and Training

Please see the I:DNA.eu website

https://i-dna.eu/

for a growing library of templates, example documents, articles, white-papers and training.

www.ingramcontent.com/pod-product-compliance
Lightning Source LLC
Chambersburg PA
CBHW050112210326
41519CB00015BA/3930